# THE WORST CARS EVER SOLD

# THE WORST CARS EVER SOLD

## GILES CHAPMAN

The
History
Press

First published in the United Kingdom in 2001 as
The Worst Cars Ever Sold in Britain by
Sutton Publishing Limited

The hardback edition reprinted in 2002 (twice),
2003 (twice)

Paperback edition first published in 2006
Reprinted 2007

Reprinted in 2008 by
The History Press
The Mill, Brimscombe Port,
Stroud, Gloucestershire, GL5 2QG
www.thehistorypress.co.uk

British Library Cataloguing
in Publication Data
A catalogue record for this
book is available from the
British Library.

ISBN 978-0-7509-4714-5

Typeset in 9.5/13.5pt Helvetica.
Typesetting and origination by Sutton Publishing Limited.
Printed and bound in England.

# CONTENTS

Introduction      7

The Cars      8

League Tables      148

# INTRODUCTION

I seem to get a lot of phone calls from people seeking arcane bits of motoring information – part of my career is built on supplying it. But it's not often I get the chance to put all my favourite bits into one book . . . and then liberally sprinkle it with mischief and irony.

It's not easy. True, I had files and files on some of these vehicles – there are 70 in all – which I've been quietly adding to for 25 years, squirrelling away nuggets of information, press cuttings, interviews, quotes, sales literature and photographs in the vague belief that they would, one day, 'be useful'.

However, when it comes to hard-to-find facts and figures for a project like this, you don't have the car industry on your side. The car industry does not like talk of failure, and many of the cars you'll read about in the following pages have been swept under the carpet by those responsible. It's a rare PR man who'll lower his guard and admit that, yes, that particular car was a clunker. Several have, however, and I thank them without embarrassing them by name.

Bad cars: they don't really make them any more, do they? No, is the straight answer. There's scarcely a car on sale in the UK today that I wouldn't happily drive across Europe; I would be secure in the knowledge that it would get me there in comfort, safety and style.

But it wasn't like that a generation ago. A large minority of new cars had to be approached with grave reservations in mind, or else avoided altogether. I've gathered many of them here that I trust will strike a note with you.

On the other hand, I also secretly hope that you violently disagree with me. These are *my* idea of bad cars – there was no committee involved – and I happily admit to not having driven, or even seen, them all. If you want to have it out with me about any of these three- or four-wheeled unfortunates – and have some facts or anecdotes with which to challenge me – then I relish getting a letter.

Finally, no matter how bad the cars are in this book, I'm glad they existed. My vision of Car Hell would contain solely beautiful Ferraris, magnificent Mercedes-Benzes and efficient Volkswagen Golfs. The worst cars ever sold in Britain have provided me with so much intrigue, debate and fun that, really, I'm inexplicably fond and protective of all of them.

*Giles Chapman*

# THE AC PETITE
## AT A GLANCE

**Built:** 1952–58 in Thames Ditton, Surrey
**Engine:** single-cylinder, 346/353cc
**Top speed:** 40mph
**Price when new:** £255
**Number produced:** 4,000 approx

## ON THE MINUS SIDE

No wheelarch apertures in those slabby little sides seems to hint at four wheels – when, in fact, there's only three – and a puncture in a MkI is a major palaver. The Petite certainly offers you a driving 'experience': whether it's one you'd actually enjoy, however, is another matter entirely.

# SAVING MONEY THE GRIM WAY IN AC'S BOXY LITTLE TRIKE

A C, originally standing for Auto Carriers, is Britain's oldest independent car maker. It's just celebrated its centenary, and continues to make the revived AC Cobra at a factory based near the historic former race track at Brooklands. But here's a car the like of which, while possibly more successful in terms of numbers sold, will never again figure in the company's range.

The Petite was a tiny economy car made from 1952 until 1958 in Thames Ditton, Surrey and, thanks to AC's sporting reputation, its maker managed to flog thousands of them. It could touch 70mpg.

While it looked like a mobile slab of fruit cake, there was room for a small family inside, and 'power' came from a two-stroke Villiers motorbike engine in the back, 346 and later, in

Doreen Waterworth and son Christopher enjoying the simple pleasures of their AC Petite, in the front garden.

AC's three-wheelers may have sold well but the company, now over 100 years old, is more famous for making sports cars like this Cobra.

Those three little wheels are tucked away for 'aerodynamic' reasons – just don't have a puncture without your toolkit to hand.

a MkII version, 353cc. Belts activated a three-speed-and-reverse gearbox and wheels – on the MkI, spoked motorbike ones at the back and a tiny 12in scooter one at the front, so no spare was carried – were independently sprung. Bodywork was steel and aluminium.

Lancashire motorist Derek Waterworth owned one in the 1950s, and here it is with his wife Doreen and son Christopher. Like many similar owners, he ran a motorbike until Christopher came along, but the fact the baby's cot sat directly over the Petite's raucous engine never led to tears, apparently.

The Petite was one of a flotilla of 'light cars' that prospered during the Suez fuel crisis years but were seen off by the Mini in 1959. AC three-wheelers, though, remained prominent in our roadscape: it made thousands of those ubiquitous light blue invalid cars for the NHS.

## ON THE PLUS SIDE

Classic ACs don't come cheap – the Ace and the Cobra are among the most sought-after British sports cars of all time. So the Petite, if you can find a surviving example, offers an affordable entrée into the world of AC. And compared to some rival microcars, it was quite refined.

**Built**: 1984–86 in Naples, Italy
**Engine**: flat four-cylinder, 1186/1490cc
**Top speed**: 108mph (1.5Ti)
**Price when new**: £5,590 (1.5Ti)
**Number produced**: 61,750

## ON THE MINUS SIDE

Well, you have a choice: you can go for either the horrible Nissan styling, with all of its image drawbacks, or you can choose the awful Alfa Romeo quality, and the endless annoying things that crack, rot, fall off or fizzle out. Either way, it's one small hatchback to avoid.

# JOINT-VENTURE JALOPY WAS A CLASH OF CULTURES ALL ROUND

When times are hard, people resort to desperate measures. And like an aristocrat reduced to selling timeshare apartments, the once-proud Milanese firm of Alfa Romeo was really up against it in the early 1980s. It was owned by the Italian state, but the investment it badly needed to replace the much-liked Alfasud and its other old faithfuls was not forthcoming from the weary government bureaucrats.

So a corporate marriage with Nissan appeared to offer a dream solution. The 1984 Arna was the first born.

This transplanted the front suspension, engine and gearbox of the Alfasud into the body of the Nissan Cherry. The car was assembled at Alfa's plant near Naples and sold in Europe as either the Alfa Romeo Arna or the Nissan Cherry Europe. Apart from the differing company insignia, they were identical.

It looks just like a Nissan Cherry but the Alfa Romeo wheels give the game away – this is the Arna, in this case the four-door SL.

The Arna in three-door 1.5Ti form – no great shakes in the looks department but still, allegedly, brimming with Alfasud-style verve.

## ON THE PLUS SIDE

Well, you have a choice: you can go for either the thoroughly practical and user-friendly Nissan detail design, or you can choose the excellent Alfa Romeo 'boxer' engines, whose performance and verve never fail to tingle the enthusiastic spine. Either way, it's a fascinating piece of forgotten motoring history.

Alfa purists hated the ugly shape and typically Japanese interior of the car but, because it was lighter than the Alfasud, it happened to be rather quicker – especially in 1.5Ti form – with handling not much worse than its illustrious forebear. Nissan diehards, by contrast, preferred their economy motoring to be supplied from quality-conscious Japan, and not slapdash old Italy.

So it was never what you'd call popular, despite the choice of three or five doors, and a plan to build a jointly developed off-roader was soon shelved. After less than five years the marriage was over: Fiat bought the ailing Alfa Romeo and hoisted the all-Italian flag above it once more. Nissan built its own factory in Sunderland. And the Arna was quietly consigned to the dustbin of history. Which, really, was no bad thing.

More mixed messages: the horrible black plastic dashboard is courtesy of Nissan, the sporty three-spoke steering wheel from Alfa Romeo – Arna SL again.

## THE ALLARD CLIPPER
### AT A GLANCE

**Built:** 1953–55 in Clapham, south-west London

**Engine:** two-cylinder, 346cc

**Top speed:** unknown

**Price when new:** £267

**Number produced:** 20 (estimated)

### ON THE MINUS SIDE

Rally hero Sydney Allard knew he was on to, er, a loser despite his worthy intention to put the impecunious on wheels. It's just a surprise he didn't realise from the start that a mere 346cc and one tiny wheel were always going to have trouble transporting five people.

# TELL SYD; THIS AIN'T THE WAY TO BRING MOTORING TO THE MASSES

Sydney Allard, bespectacled garage owner and sports car maker from Clapham, south-west London, won the 1952 Monte Carlo Rally, the only man to do so in a car of his own design. The only reason more people don't remember this is that King George VI was inconsiderate enough to die at the same moment.

But even as the champagne corks flew in Monaco, fast cars from big companies, especially Jaguar, with their superior refinement and performance, were obliterating sales of small-time specials like Allards.

Sydney's answer was to attack the other end of the market – with the ultimate economy car. He employed a young engineer called David Gottlieb to design it and a firm called Hordern-Richmond Ltd to make its plastic body, making it among the earliest glassfibre car shells.

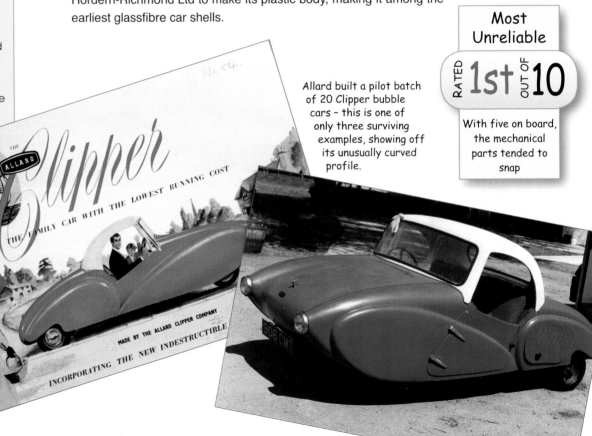

Brochure artwork for Sydney Allard's economy car; the graphic artist took considerable licence in making the car vast and its occupants tiny.

Allard built a pilot batch of 20 Clipper bubble cars – this is one of only three surviving examples, showing off its unusually curved profile.

### Most Unreliable
RATED **1st** OUT OF **10**

With five on board, the mechanical parts tended to snap

What resulted was one of the oddest-looking British bubble cars ever, a tiny ovular contraption that could seat three abreast in cramped discomfort and a further two, undoubtedly nervous, children in 'dickey seats' behind when the boot was converted.

An 8bhp 346cc Villiers twin motorbike engine powered the car via its nearside rear wheel. But cooling difficulties and weak driveshafts meant the Clipper, besides looking ludicrous, was also hopelessly unreliable.

A pilot batch of about 20 was made but, despite Syd's exhortation to parents to 'Take the nipper in a Clipper', real production never began.

Today, there are just three survivors, including one in Germany and this one – which, according to owner Graham Deakin, was apparently so undesirable it had nine owners between 1955 and '62. That total included one garage that had it returned three times by disgruntled buyers!

## ON THE PLUS SIDE

An unlikely pioneer of glassfibre in car bodies, the Clipper has a strange allure for lovers of motoring failure, and that multi-curved little mollusc of a shape does raise a grin – and not a little respect for a decently intentioned attempt to brighten up a grey 1950s motoring landscape.

Worst Selling

RATED **5th** OUT OF **10**

Number Sold: 20

There's no boot under that plastic lid: pull the handle and two additional 'dickey'-style kids' seats are revealed, ideal for the sadistic parent.

**Built**: 1975–80 in Kenosha, Wisconsin, USA

**Engine**: six-cylinder, 3799/4235cc; V8, 4979cc

**Top speed**: 104mph (3.8-litre)

**Price when new**: £4,758

**Number produced**: 280,000 approx

# AMERICAN MOTORS' OFFBEAT ADVENTURE IN 1970S MINIMALISM

In the fuel crisis of the mid-1970s American car makers were stymied. General Motors, Ford, Chrysler and American Motors Corporation just did not make small, economical cars. They could only look on aghast as Japanese imports piled in and snatched their sales.

The panic to compete sired some emergency products. The Ford Pinto, which later developed a tendency to self-combust; the Plymouth Cricket, a hastily imported and 'Americanised' Hillman Avenger; and, of course, the AMC Pacer.

Ah, the Pacer! In living memory, few new cars have received such derision upon their debut. Britain's *Motor*

The Pacer, originally intended as a showcase for rotary engine technology, when new in 1976 – it was shorter than a Caddy but just as wide.

**Ugliest**
RATED **1st** OUT OF **10**

Goldfish bowl on wheels that's bigger than a Granada

Optional Indian-pattern, Basketry-print upholstery and massive amounts of headroom made the Pacer's interior an even odder place to be.

## ON THE MINUS SIDE

The Pacer was designed as a technology showcase, the 'first wide small car', with a Wankel rotary engine. But the engine never appeared and the intriguing concept went downhill immediately. The Pacer is a car that does no one thing well, looks absolutely ludicrous, and is awful to drive.

magazine, for instance, brazenly announced on its cover 'We test the Pacer – and wish we hadn't'.

In photographs, the goldfish-bowl looks and three doors suggested a car that was about the size of a Volkswagen Polo. In the metal, it was longer than a Ford Granada, with the huge wheels of every other Detroit dinosaur.

As it was an economy model, you probably expected a thrifty engine. But the smallest available in the Pacer was a burly six-cylinder 3.8-litre motor as big as a Jaguar's.

It did boast a driver's door longer than the passenger's for easy access to the rear seats. But even that novelty went rather pear-shaped when cars were converted to right-hand drive for the UK.

The Pacer Wagon estate was introduced in 1978 but even its increased versatility couldn't help stave off the car's demise.

The Pacer utterly failed to stave off the Toyota Corolla and its economical ilk and lasted for a miserable five years before AMC quietly snuffed it out, although it made a starring return in the movie comedy *Wayne's World* and its sequel. Today, if you own an Edsel, then a perfectly preserved Pacer makes an ideal companion. . . .

Spotted in a garden in the East Midlands recently, here's proof that a few strange souls decided to buy the handful of right-hand drive Pacers.

Daftest Features

RATED **1st** OUT OF **10**

Doors are different sizes, fine in the USA but impractical on right-hand drive cars

**Built**: 1958–68 in Birmingham, West Midlands

**Engine**: four-cylinder, 2199cc petrol, 2178cc diesel

**Top speed**: 60mph approx, depending on specification

**Price when new**: £650

**Number produced**: 21,000 approx

Slowest

RATED **4th** OUT OF **10**

Max speed:
60 mph

# MUM WAS RIGHT: DON'T PLAY WITH THE GIPSIES IN THE WOOD

**W**hen Austin announced its four-wheel drive Gipsy on 28 February 1958, it thought it had a winner: a rugged Land-Rover beater that, thanks to a revolutionary rubber suspension, would be gentler on driver and passengers.

Ten years later, however, the Gipsy bowed out with a whimper, having been no more than a thorn in the side of its Solihull rival.

Intended as a replacement for Austin's strictly military Champ scout car, the company's engineers sealed the Gipsy's fate by building it with a steel chassis *and* a steel body, and inadequate corrosion protection meant hard-used Gipsys soon became off-road rust-buckets; Land-Rovers were built mainly from rot-proof aluminium.

The Gipsy's unique, independent 'Flexitor' trailing arm rubber suspension, meanwhile, gave a smooth and comfortable ride. But the chassis-mounted differentials had to take all

An early example of the Austin Gipsy, amply demonstrating its off-road capability while its Flexitor rubber suspension cushions the driver.

## ON THE MINUS SIDE

Tough-looking off-roaders have got to actually be tough, and the Gipsy – which looked like a Land-Rover rip-off on the outside – was weak in all the wrong places. Swamps caused it to rust, boulders knocked the stuffing out of it, and that daft name can't have helped.

the pounding, creating a terrible reputation for wear and damage. In 1962, conventional springs with beam axles became optional, and by 1965 the Flexitor system was deleted for good – the beam axles could lift the differentials, with the axle, above the bumps, and reduced the turning circle from 42 to 35ft.

It was built in three progressively improved series, but who actually bought them? Few Brits: most were sold to unsuspecting armies in places like Malaysia, and to export markets like Switzerland and Australia.

A fire at the Birmingham factory that built them, almost to order, in 1963 curtailed supplies, and the Gipsy never recovered in its tussle with Land-Rover. Austin's publicity stunts, like driving one up the side of a dam in Nairobi, or to the summit of Ben Nevis, were diverting but fruitless.

After several mergers, the Austin Gipsy and the Land-Rover were thrown together, in 1968, in the British Leyland colossus. The Gipsy, naturally, was almost the first victim of rationalisation.

*The Gipsy liked nothing more than hauling a trailer-load of milk churns, although many pursued a military lifestyle, often abroad.*

**Most Handy**

RATED **1st** OUT OF **10**

Comfortable off-road alternative to a Land-Rover

## ON THE PLUS SIDE

Let's face it, Land-Rovers are 10-a-penny, and the early Gipsy, with its smooth-riding rubber suspension, was a revelation. The last examples were well-sorted too, with an eye-widening variety of bodies and uses. Austin was an early pioneer of today's craze for 'recreational' off-roaders.

**Daftest Features**

RATED **2nd** OUT OF **10**

Rubber suspension failed to take all of the punishment

*This is a 1958 short-wheelbase version but the Gipsy came in three progressively improved series, and with a wide variety of bodywork.*

**Built**: 1973–83 in Longbridge, Birmingham

**Engine**: four-cylinder, 998/1098/1275/1485/1748cc

**Top speed**: 100mph

**Price when new**: from £974

**Number produced**: 642,350

# ALL-AGGRO THAT TURNED TO GRUDGING AFFECTION

The Austin Allegro is fast becoming a collector's item. True, it'll be a few years before they turn up at Sotheby's auctions, but people who love them – and there are two thriving owners' clubs – swear by them.

It's a far cry from the mid-1970s, when owners usually swore at them. When new, the Allegro was unloved.

The car had a tough act to follow, the Austin/ Morris 1100 and 1300 – for most of the 1960s, Britain's best-selling motor car. And, to be fair, British Leyland tried to come up with an advanced replacement: the Allegro featured innovative Hydragas suspension, and went for a rounded look where the 1100 had been almost brutally straitlaced.

Thing was, what looked good in the mind's eye of the designer – in this case a mild-mannered chap called Harris Mann – turned out dumpy and unappealing in the metal. The hunchbacked Allegro looked as though it should

The Allegro's 'quartic' steering wheel was soon replaced.

The Vanden Plas version of the Allegro, made from 1974 until 1980, was strange-looking but at least boasted a hand-finished interior.

'Can you see yourself in one of those?'
'No'.
Mr and Mrs Average seen here in 1973 weighing up the pros and cons of the new Allegro.

Best Selling
RATED 7th OUT OF 10
Sold: 642,350

## ON THE MINUS SIDE

Slug-like looks and patchy quality made the early Allegro the bane of its customers' lives – and British Leyland a laughing stock. Worse, BL hedged its bets by making an alternative small family car for the more old-farty buyer. This was the Morris Marina – if anything, a worse all-rounder than the Allegro itself!

conceal a useful hatchback, but didn't. And the car's 'quartic' steering wheel was so obviously gimmicky it was replaced after just two years by a normal round one.

Where the 1100 had sharp handling, the gas-sprung Allegro was a bouncy castle of a drive. Legendary early customer complaints also included rear windows that popped out under hard acceleration.

All of which wouldn't, perhaps, have been so bad if the car's quality was A1. But it was caught in the thick of British Leyland's appalling labour relations, and the badly screwed-together, unreliable Allegro was one of the major reasons why British people started to buy Japanese cars or, if not, Fords.

In its twilight years, the Allegro's bugbears were chased away. The last ones were probably good cars if anyone bothered to find out.

And, ironically, where the 'All Aggro' once engendered little more than a sneer, survivors – and there are quite a few because, like giant, motorised cockroaches, they are resistant to natural destruction – are cherished. Some models are even on the 'danger' list of extinction. If you own a 1973 1750SS or Sport TC, for instance, you could be sitting on (a very small amount of) gold dust. . . .

The 1976 Allegro estate, although spacious, was another own-goal in the looks department.

## ON THE PLUS SIDE

Well, the sight of an Allegro nearly always brings a smile – the psychological impact of a curvy car from a straight-lined era, perhaps? And later examples are pretty reliable and rust-resistant. Today's owners are beguiled by their Allegros, and the car's rising kitsch factor means fewer and fewer are being scrapped.

**Built**: 1964–73 in Ellesmere Port,
Merseyside and Folkestone, Kent
**Engine**: four-cylinder, 1057/1159/1256cc
**Top speed**: 75mph approx
**Price when new**: £624
**Number produced**: unknown

### ON THE MINUS SIDE

This is a van with windows,
there's no getting
around it. As there was
precious little extra
sound-deadening, it's
an uncivilised ride for
all concerned, and the
interior is spartan. The
Beagle was a real make-
do-and-mend machine,
in the true British tradition,
and rusts a treat.

# BEDFORD BEAGLE; HOUNDED OUT OF THE MODERN WORLD

The phrase 'Bedford HA van' is unlikely to ring many bells, except with a few commercial vehicle anoraks. But if you were to picture a typical Post Office Telephones van of the 1970s, then it's this trusty little vehicle you would summon up in your mind.

Boxy, basic, bright yellow, and usually sporting a ladder on the roof, thousands of them were bought by the Post Office for its telephone repairmen. Many more went to other fleets and small businesses, making local deliveries all over the country.

The little HA was introduced in 1964, a humdrum van version of the Vauxhall Viva car, with which it shared engines and a rear-drive layout. It wasn't exciting, just highly practical, and it continued to be manufactured at Vauxhall's Merseyside factory until as late as 1983. It was big orders like the ones from Post Office Telephones that kept it going so long, latterly as a very cheap vehicle indeed, although its successor British Telecom decided it needed something more up-to-date.

There was no Vauxhall Viva estate but Vauxhall sanctioned a Kent company called Martin Walter – most famous for its

Most Handy

RATED **2nd** OUT OF **10**

Bit of a hound in the looks department but a useful runabout

No frills: the Bedford Beagle was little more than an HA van with side windows and a rear seat, even though it emanated from the Dormobile factory.

Dormobile campers – to create one from the HA van. So in went side windows with a sliding section, a folding rear seat, and a contrasting colour stripe along the side. They called it the Bedford Beagle.

It was practical and thrifty but crude and noisy – the antithesis of a modern equivalent like a Renault Kangoo – and sold in tiny numbers to style-free drivers who were more concerned about their dogs or cargo than everyday driving pleasure.

This is how you'll remember the Bedford HA (if you recall it at all, that is): Post Office Telephones, now BT, bought thousands for its repairmen.

## ON THE PLUS SIDE

Here was a practical, easy-driving little holdall that was perfect for anyone who rates mechanical simplicity and a lack of frippery. With its two, side-hinged doors and square-cut profile, getting stuff in and out was easy, and the uncomplicated Viva basis means reliability was a watchword.

Same story, different ending: the Beagle, like the Bedford HA, was based on the Viva, Vauxhall's conventional small car answer to the Mini.

**Built**: 1957–58 in Preston, Lancashire

**Engine**: single-cylinder, 197cc

**Top speed**: 60mph

**Price when new**: £350

**Number produced**: 1,800 approx

### ON THE MINUS SIDE

Motoring doesn't get much more basic than a Bond Minicar. Fortunately, they're too gutless to get most drivers into trouble, but the MkE's, ahem, slight unsteadiness could catch out the most wary of drivers. Minimal in every way, you'll give up long before the car does.

# MINIMAL MOTORING THAT MIGHT JUST TRIP YOU UP

If Valerie Johnston – described in this picture's caption as 'rally driver and secretary . . . of West Wickham, Kent' – is reading this, she'll be 64 today. One wonders how she felt at being drafted in to publicise the Bond Minicar MkE in 1957.

She probably didn't realise the fifth model in this venerable series only just avoided a reputation as a deathtrap.

Since 1948, the utilitarian three-wheelers had emerged from a Preston, Lancashire factory to a concept drawn up by eccentric jobbing engineer Lawrie Bond.

He reasoned that, by using a tiny 122cc Villiers two-stroke single-cylinder engine and the most lightweight materials, you could offer personal transport to make every gallon of precious, post-war petrol go as far as possible. The first Bond Minicar MkAs were so basic they didn't even have rear suspension.

At £198, however, and taxed like a motorbike, it was a winner, and thousands of Minicars soon pottered away at the front of slow-moving traffic jams.

By 1957, though, despite improvements and 75cc more, it looked austere. So Bond planned the MkE to be longer, roomier for passengers and luggage, and much more car-like.

But the prototype showed an alarming tendency to topple over on corners. Its physical geometry had been misjudged, and several inches had to be chopped out of its wheelbase to stabilise it, and the rear track was widened – the afterthought bulging wheelarches are the visual giveaway.

Hardly a car for budding rally drivers, or sensible secretaries, and a properly re-designed MkF replaced it in 1959. The last Minicar was made in 1966, by when 24,484 had been sold to Britain's motoring misers.

The earlier Minicars, like this 1953-vintage MkC, were even weirder, with their dummy front wings – compensated for by a tiny turning circle.

RATED **5th** OUT OF **10**

Slowest

Max speed: 60 mph

Valerie Johnston, are you out there? The Wickham secretary and rally driver tries the MkE Minicar – but watch that corner ahead, Val. . . .

## ON THE PLUS SIDE

As Bill Clinton once famously said: 'It's the economy, stupid'. If you're a hardy soul and you like personal transport – out of the rain – for the most meagre of money then the Minicar is right up your street. It has period charm, and a rabidly fanatical owners' club into which you will be sucked.

**Built**: 1930–33 in Maidenhead, Berkshire

**Engine**: eight-cylinder, 2956cc

**Top speed**: 85mph

**Price when new**: £1,500

**Number produced**: 12

Most
Unreliable

RATED **2nd** OUT OF **10**

Badly cooled engine
meant the long tail
could catch fire

# A SLIPPERY CUSTOMER WITH A STING IN ITS TAIL

It should come as no surprise to learn that this blimpish-looking device was the work of the splendidly named Sir Dennistoun Burney. He was the prosperous and tireless inventor, and ex-Unionist MP, whose R100 airship designs had excited the world (until, that is, the later R101 plummeted tragically from the sky in 1930, killing 48 people).

Undeterred, Burney decided to deploy his aerodynamic skills 'to show that a properly streamlined car would score over its more conventional competitors'.

The fabric-covered body frame of his Burney Streamline was constructed fuselage-style. Completely flat underneath, it was a sort of inverted truss steel girder, cross-braced by strainer wires.

Suspension was all-round independent but the Alvis engine used in an early prototype was too weak to power the slug-like

## ON THE MINUS SIDE

Is there any synergy between aircraft and car design? Not if the Burney Streamline is a test case. Too big, too complicated and lacking in the essentials – like engine cooling – that are so important to land-based vehicles. Despite regal patronage, Sir Dennistoun's dream car was really a daft idea.

Sir Dennistoun Burney's extraordinary, aerodynamic motor car, designed with airship principles in mind and patronised by royalty.

## ON THE PLUS SIDE

How wonderful that there are single-minded individuals willing to push the boundaries of design and create cars like the Streamline. Despite its faults, the Burney was a fantastic attempt to explore new aerodynamic ground, and well endowed with technical innovations. Maybe with a front-mounted engine, it could have taken off.

behemoth – it had seating for seven – so a Beverley Barnes straight-eight twin-cam motor powered most of the 'production' Streamlines.

This lived in a casing tacked on to the car's anteater tail and was prone to overheating. Despite twin air scoops sucking air to its lateral radiators, engines often caught fire.

One novel feature was spare wheels housed inside the rear doors, and the car was supposed to handle quite well despite its enormous length. It could, reputedly, kiss 80mph.

The Prince of Wales was a notable patron of Burney's Streamline Cars, based in Maidenhead, but just a dozen of the high-tech monsters found buyers – at a correspondingly colossal £1,500.

Manchester's Crossley car company took it over in 1933 but, even with their robust 2-litre engine six-cylinder engine and the price halved, only 25 more were sold.

An alternative bodystyle, with a more conventional nose, didn't solve the Burney Streamline's big problem: catching fire when the engine got hot.

Worst Selling
RATED **3rd** OUT OF **10**
Number Sold: 12

**Built**: 1970–80 in Poissy, Paris, France, and also assembled in Madrid, Spain
**Engine**: four-cylinder, 1812cc
**Top speed**: 101mph
**Price when new**: £1,498
**Number produced**: unknown

### ON THE MINUS SIDE

Partly Humber, partly Simca, some of them made in Spain, all of them desperately tedious to drive, the Chrysler 180's genesis is, by the standards of today's switched-on car industry, a masterpiece of ineptness. And driving it was an eye-opener – few European cars have been such a charisma-free zone.

# THE SHOULD-HAVE-BEEN HUMBER THAT EVERYONE IGNORED

The Chrysler 180 is one of the great unloved cars of modern times, a model so devastatingly mediocre and unmemorable that few knew about it even when it was still on sale.

If you think it looks a bit like a scaled-up Hillman Avenger then you'd be right: it was designed in Britain by the same team, and was originally meant to be sold as a Humber. However, the old Rootes Group logic was thrown out by its new owner Chrysler Corporation, which was keen to get its name better known in Europe. The American masters therefore gave the job of designing the car's powertrain to its French subsidiary Simca, and decreed the history book be torn up and the car launched as the first European Chrysler.

*Is it a Humber? Is it a Simca? Well, it's a bit of both, but called a Chrysler. Few noticed the 180 when it was new, so don't fret about not recognising it.*

As an Anglo-French product with a Yankee name, then, the car had a bit of an identity crisis. More worrying, though, was its complete lack of driver appeal, with soggy handling and gutless performance, and a tacky, US-inspired look both inside and out.

There was an even slower 1.6 model, thankfully confined to France, and a later 2-litre with a bit more poke. Some 23,000 2-litres were sold, with maybe twice as many 180s shifted in 10 years, no-one's sure.

Amazingly, it would be five years until another Chrysler, the Alpine, was unveiled. A year on and all Hillmans and Simcas became Chryslers too, although the name vanished in Europe after Chrysler sold its British and French bits to Peugeot, allegedly for just $1 – plus debts. And the Chrysler 180 ended its obscure life as the even more obscure Talbot 180.

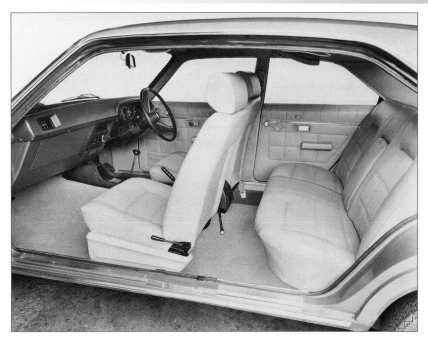

Inside the executive car no-one knows: lots of space and, no doubt, comfy seats but precious little in the way of charisma in the Chrysler 180.

## ON THE PLUS SIDE

We included this section of the book to offer some counter-balance to my unrelentingly brutal criticism. So here goes: the Chrysler 180 has four doors, four wheels, a roof to keep the rain off, an engine to make it go and brakes to make it stop. It's all right, -ish.

In 1973 came the Chrysler 2-litre, with extra equipment, more power and a vinyl roof. Granada man, however, expressed even less interest.

# DEFINITELY NOT THE JEWEL IN CITROËN'S CROWN

In the shadow of the home of the Mars Bar on the Trading Estate in Slough, Buckinghamshire, Citroën had a British factory. For years, it had bolted together its Traction Avant cars here in order to qualify them as 'British-made' for taxation purposes. And, between 1953 and 1959, it also churned out a British version of its rustic 2CV.

To make this bizarre car acceptable to British eyes, Citroën fitted chrome bumpers and hubcaps, covered the hammock-type seats in plaid cloth, and stuck a badge on the front that stated 'Citroën Front Drive'.

Buyers, it must be said, were not persuaded by this piece of information. They stayed away in droves. They bought nice, normal Standard Eights and Austin A30s instead.

So, in a last-ditch attempt to force the 425cc, two-cylinder 2CV on us, Citroën produced a uniquely British 2CV. The 1959 Bijou featured a 2CV chassis with a smart new glassfibre body from the drawing board of Peter Kirwan-Taylor – the stylist of one of the best-looking contemporary new cars, the Lotus Elite, even though he actually pursued a career as an accountant.

Slowest
RATED **3rd** OUT OF **10**
Max speed: 50 mph

One of the 200 or so Bijous made in Slough – the whole front of the car hinged forward for access to the Citroën 2CV flat twin-cylinder engine.

Alas, the handiwork was fine but the Bijou turned out to be rather heavier than the original, pressed-tin, puny 2CV, and consequently even slower. Worse than that for Citroën, the new Mini undercut the £674 Bijou. In five years, just 207 of this, the only Citroën ever designed outside France, were sold.

But it was not quite the end for the Deux Chevaux in Britain: the country happily took to the 2CV when it was re-introduced in 1974 . . . at the height of a fuel crisis.

The traditional 'tin snail' Citroën 2CV was perceived as too raw for British tastes, hence the Bijou. Yet the original was a hit during the 1970s fuel crisis.

THE UNIQUE CITROEN *BIJOU*

## ON THE PLUS SIDE

The 2CV, bless its heart, is not strong on creature comforts. The Bijou, however, offered the French car's laudable economy and ride in a neat British package. Plus, one of the 2CV's intrinsic problems is rust and the Bijou, being constructed from glassfibre, is never likely to do that.

Front cover of the sales brochure depicts the Bijou as a housewife's favourite, happy to potter about on the daily chores in a suburban utopia.

# NO MATTER HOW IT WAS DRESSED UP, THE DENEM WAS PANTS

It doesn't matter how dull a motor car becomes to novelty-hungry European eyes: there is always likely to be a market for it somewhere. So it is that spent-force models we thought had limped off this mortal coil have often, in fact, sneaked away for a new life in far-flung places.

The Renault 12, for instance, was a terminally tedious, albeit mostly very dependable, machine last made in its homeland of France in 1980.

However, it has survived and indeed flourished in Romania as the Dacia. The Romanians started assembling 12s in 1970 with the beaming approval of the murderous dictator Nicolae Ceausescu. But, while France progressed to other, more exciting models, Dacia saw no reason to change.

## ON THE MINUS SIDE

The British sales offensive lasted for less than a year, so unless you need a hire car in Romania, encountering a Dacia is rare. During the grim Ceausescu era, Dacia quality control didn't exist, and the cars were appallingly made. If you want this sort of thing, search out a Renault original.

The Dacia Denem was nothing more than a Renault 12 laid low by Romanian build quality. It was advertised as 'Very Acceptable', but wasn't.

Indeed, the Dacia has mutated, like a seeded onion in the Eastern European sunshine, into forms never imagined by Renault designers: there are now pick-up, van, hatchback and even coupé versions of the 12. And if you thought the original looked unenticing, you should see how hideous it looks now.

A half-baked plan to import the car to the UK in 1982 was an abject failure – apart from a small fleet which was, until recently, in service with the Romanian embassy in London's Kensington diplomatic district.

The British importer came up with what it thought a cool name for the car – the Dacia Denem. And the advertising campaign didn't help much: the car was touted to potential buyers as the 'Very Acceptable Dacia Denem'. Amazing the Advertising Standards Authority wasn't called in, really. Few were sold, although later a small consignment of Renault 12-based Dacia pick-ups also found its way here.

## ON THE PLUS SIDE

Few cars are as shoddy as a Dacia, yet the basic Renault 12 design was pretty good in 1970. The saloon was roomy, the estate useful. You still sometimes see them in the UK, so owners must be on to a good thing, or else eking the last drop out of their motoring.

the very acceptable **Denem**

A second attempt to bring Dacias to the UK saw this Renault 12-based one-ton pick-up foisted on the British tradesman; of course, he resisted it.

**Built**: 1958–75 in Eindhoven, Holland
**Engine**: two-cylinder, 600cc/746cc
**Top speed**: 60mph
**Price when new**: £813
**Number produced**: 280,082

# HASSLE-FREE TRUNDLING FOR YOUR TIMID AUNT MABEL

A decent small automatic was something of a Holy Grail for car makers in the 1950s. They were convinced that what was often referred to as 'two-pedal motoring' could open up the world of car ownership to many new buyers.

So it was a surprise in 1958 when a Dutch manufacturer of trucks and trailers beat the big guns. Moreover, Daf's crisp-looking Daffodil came only with automatic transmission.

The system was called Variomatic, and was the forerunner of today's CVT gearboxes. In effect, there was only one forward and one reverse 'speed', infinitely variable drive being taken to the rear wheels by stepless toothed rubber belts in a V-formation. And, of course, no clutch or clutch pedal.

Power, such as it was, came from a flat-twin-cylinder, 600cc, air-cooled engine, meaning a maximum of 60mph. But the car wasn't intended as a motorway pounder, more a smart town runabout aimed at – if Daf's advertising was to be believed – Audrey Hepburn-type gals with white gloves on and no intention of ever driving anything more demanding.

Oddly enough, it was the Dutch who pointed the way to today's small automatic cars with the 1958 launch of the Daf Daffodil.

### ON THE MINUS SIDE

Daf at least promised a car that was easy to drive, even if it was slow and weedy. This was a machine for motoring dunces, with a lever to push one way for forwards and another for backwards. In the motoring pecking order, this is a Zimmer frame to the Mini's in-line skate.

In truth, its appeal lay among pensioners and those too timid ever to master a manual gearbox and the Daf Daffodil, soon known as the 750 with a larger engine, and then from 1967 as the 33, spawned a family of sister models like the 44, 55 and 66. In 14 years, the basic version sold an impressive 280,000.

Daf off-loaded its car division to Volvo in 1975 and for a short time the Daf 66 was rebadged the Volvo 66. The hassle-free automatic dream lives on today in the S/V40, made in the same Dutch factory.

This is what it was all about: no gearlever and just two pedals made the little Daf absolutely the simplest car in the world to drive.

Slowest
RATED **6th** OUT OF **10**

Max speed:
60 mph

## ON THE PLUS SIDE

In a congested world, we're waking up to small automatics and the Daf was the pioneer of them all. In thorough Dutch style, it was neatly designed and well-built, and probably played its part in helping a stratum of sensible 1960s motorists take the wheel for the first time.

With a neater front and various other mods, the basic Daf lasted until 1975 – just a year before Volvo bought the firm for its automatic expertise.

# YOU CAN RELY ON A DATSUN SUNNY – TO BORE YOU RIGID

In 1973, one in 20 new cars sold in the UK was a Datsun. The British motor industry – happy in its cosy insularity – was, understandably, most alarmed. People could make all the jokes they liked about yellow peril, and how the 'Made in Japan' label was a euphemism for tin-pot. But, when it came to Japanese cars like Datsuns, the British public just couldn't get enough.

Keith Hopkins, managing director of British Leyland's Austin Morris division in the early 1970s, recalls Japanese cars had three things on their side – they were reliable, available, and everything came as standard.

'These were cars that had a radio when even a heater was extra on an Austin,' he recalls.

Squadrons of cars like this Datsun Sunny 120Y coupé, ugly, plasticky and cramped though they were, purred out of the showroom. It wasn't a car to drive quickly despite its sporty moniker – the 120Y's road manners were dire. However, it started on the button every morning and nothing ever fell off. 'The Japanese thought that was what mattered', says Hopkins. 'And they were right, of course.'

In its four-year career, the 120Y notched up 2.3m sales around the world; not just as a coupé but also as a two- and four-door saloon and a handy little estate. To put that into perspective, it outsold rivals like the Austin Allegro (made for 10 years), Morris Marina (nine years) and Vauxhall Viva HC (nine years) combined.

The 120Y and its ilk were so successful in the UK that Nissan decided to build a factory in Sunderland – here's the first British-made Nissan Bluebird for export in 1988, with Tory trade minister Lord Young.

It tried to be sporty but the fastback version of the Datsun Sunny 120Y was hardly a pulse-raiser, even though it was a paragon of reliability.

No wonder the good burghers of the West Midlands metal-bashing establishment were petrified.

Indeed, the British-owned motor industry never quite recovered. But the popularity of cars like the 120Y was instrumental in bringing Nissan's factory to Sunderland.

## ON THE PLUS SIDE

A car, as many people will testify, is useless unless it can get from A to B reliably. Datsun created cars that fulfilled this simple need – something Europeans had a real problem doing. If it wasn't for cars like the Sunny, standards would never have risen to today's exceptional levels.

Here's the car the coupé was based on, the 120Y saloon – it had a radio and a heater as standard when they were costly extras on most rivals.

Those plastic wheeltrims, what are they like, eh? The Sunny coupe, like other Datsuns, was stylistically challenged but exceptional value.

## ON THE MINUS SIDE

Dull, underpowered, and with an appearance that was uncomfortable at best, and downright ugly if you were feeling uncharitable, these Datsuns lacked character, and somehow helped to dumb down the motoring world into accepting the utterly conventional. They never have, and probably never will have, a place in enthusiasts' hearts.

**Built:** 1979–95 in Worthing, West Sussex

**Engine:** a variety of four-cylinder Ford units

**Top speed:** not quantifiable

**Price when new:** £825 for basic kit

**Number produced:** unknown

Most Handy

RATED **3rd** OUT OF **10**

4x4 looks without the fuel consumption, and cheap to fix

# FORD HATED IT AND RANGE ROVER DRIVERS SIMPLY GUFFAWED

**K**it cars, Airfix-like sets of components to be assembled at home into brand new vehicles, have tended to flourish in tough times, but may have had their day now that cheap secondhand cars are so plentiful.

This was not the case in 1979 when Dutton introduced its Sierra. After a period of industrial discontent, the incoming Tory government vowed to get the country working again. But that meant several years of belt-tightening.

So the Sierra's offer of pseudo-off-roader looks for minimal cost was a big draw. It came as a glassfibre body/steel chassis unit that was all ready to accept 'donor' parts from any old Ford that had passed its sell-by date.

With some deft weekend spannering, the car could be ready to roll in days, depending on how much time and effort you put into finishing it off properly; the Sierra was basic in the extreme, and by no means all of them were well finished. The words 'arse', 'badger' and 'rough' spring to mind, not necessarily in that order.

The Sierra was probably the first 'practical' British kit – i.e. not a sports or fun car – and for many years it was the best-seller, helping Dutton reach production of 22 cars a week at one point. A legal row with Ford over use of the Sierra name also led to handy publicity, with the red-tops portraying it as a gritty David and Goliath battle.

The moment widespread prosperity returned, however, the appeal of the Sierra dropped away steeply. As the rise of real 4x4 off-roaders became unstoppable, the Dutton Sierra turned into a laughing stock.

*Just like a Range Rover – well, almost, apart from the two-wheel drive, the assorted Ford parts and the extremely variable quality.*

## ON THE MINUS SIDE

A real tough-times machine, the Sierra was a rather desperate way for hard-up motorists to create a family estate car out of motoring leftovers. Once the kit was delivered, the car's standards were in the hands of the new buyer, no matter how suspect his mechanical nous. . . .

## ON THE PLUS SIDE

Tim Dutton-Woolley, the company founder, gave thousands the chance of characterful family motoring with the passenger space and ground clearance of a Range Rover, but none of the exorbitant purchase and running costs such a car would entail. In doing that, he made a lot of people very happy.

An early design sketch for the Dutton Sierra whetted appetites for the first high-riding 'leisure' car you could build at home for peanuts.

As part of an enormous range of kit cars, Dutton offered this home-build, open-top Sierra as a consolation prize to hard-up Jeep Renegade fanciers.

There was nothing that Tim Dutton-Woolley wouldn't try – this was his Sierra-based attempt at a versatile light commercial vehicle

## THE FAIRTHORPE ATOMOTA

### AT A GLANCE

**Built**: 1958–60 in Chalfont St Peter, Buckinghamshire

**Engine**: two-cylinder, 646cc; four-cylinder, 948cc

**Top speed**: 65mph

**Price when new**: £640

**Number produced**: unknown

# DRASTIC PLASTIC FROM A FORGOTTEN HAVE-A-GO ERA

Air Vice-Marshall Donald Bennett was a most remarkable man. His Bomber Command exploits during the Second World War, which earned him his 'Pathfinder' nickname, are legendary. He also pioneered the North Atlantic ferry service – delivering new bombers to Britain – and famously walked across Norway and Sweden when he was shot down after attacking the battleship *Tirpitz*.

In peacetime, he was a front-runner in the Berlin airlift, and from 1946 to '48 ran British South American Airways. He also flirted with Liberal politics and, in philanthropic mood, in 1954 decided to build the economy car that he thought every austerity-weary British motorist longed for.

Here is what the Electron looked like in the flesh, this being an early model. Crude detail finish didn't put off impecunious speed freaks.

Slowest

RATED **9th** OUT OF **10**

Max speed: 65 mph

A brochure for the Fairthorpe Electron extolled its dynamics – the company soon abandoned economy cars in favour of cheap sportsters.

## THE Fairthorpe ELECTRON

**WONDERFUL ROAD-HOLDING, BRAKING AND SHEER SPEED**

### ON THE MINUS SIDE

Don Bennett was a Second World War giant, and an industrious chap in peace-time. A car industry tycoon he was not, and the almost unbelievably amateurish Atom and Atomota must have shocked even the most thrifty Brits. It was ration-book motoring that had no consumer future at all.

With a 650cc BSA motorbike engine at the back and lightweight plastic body, his hideous-looking Fairthorpe Atom was quite speedy but had no more creature comforts than a tough-as-nails fighter pilot might expect. The British motoring public preferred the more seemly Austin A30.

The Atomota was a much-developed version of the same car, now front-engined and with a Standard 10 power unit in the Atomota Major model. Prominent fins were grafted on to its sloping rump for a semblance of normality, but only a tiny handful of both Atoms and Atomotas was sold.

The Atomota was rapid but looked home-made, with window apertures crudely cut into its glassfibre body and exterior hinges on its doors appearing to be simply cheap, DIY hardware shop fittings.

Bennett, who died in 1986, had more luck with a later series of Fairthorpe sports cars including the Electron, Rockette and Zeta. They were effective implements for motor sport but rather inadequate as fully rounded motor cars.

## ON THE PLUS SIDE

I just love these early Fairthorpes: they were the last of a dying breed – made by have-a-go heroes who decided to make cars without any apparent aptitude for it. And they were fast: later sports models, especially the Electron Minor, gave sporting pleasure to thousands of hard-up speed freaks.

## Ugliest

RATED 2nd OUT OF 10

Homemade lash-up with crude rear fins

Rare photo of a very rare car: the Fairthorpe Atomota with rear fins inexpertly grafted on, crude plastic windows and DIY shop door hinges.

## THE FORD CONSUL CLASSIC

### AT A GLANCE

**Built:** 1961–63 in Dagenham, Essex
**Engine:** four-cylinder, 1340/1498cc
**Top speed:** 79mph
**Price when new:** £744
**Number produced:** 111,225

# A CLASSIC IN THE MAKING, FOR ALL THE WRONG REASONS

In 1961, the Ford Consul Classic was cool, really cool. Here was a car that, at the size of your dad's boring old, sit-up-and-beg car, had all the things you saw on American cars at the pictures.

Big fins at the back, four headlamps at the front under little hoods, two-tone paint, whitewall tyres, five chrome stars in the grille and that trendy rear window shape.

There were even front disc brakes – novel then – a floor-mounted gearlever (wow) and a brand new 1340cc engine.

So, how come the Classic really never caught on?

The problem, apart from the fact that it was heavy and not particularly nice to drive, was those very looks themselves. What had seemed fashionable when it was being designed

A touch of Detroit glamour in boring old England – the Ford Consul Classic was designed by Roy 'Mr Edsel' Brown but was soon out of vogue.

The pillarless, coupé version of the Classic was called the *Consul Capri*, and was a neat piece of design with an enormous boot.

## ON THE MINUS SIDE

As Ford discovered with the Puma and Vauxhall with its Tigra, if your car tries to be too fashion-conscious it risks falling out of favour all the faster. Ironically, therefore, this family Ford was a 'Classic' example of why engineers, and not style-faddists, should be running car companies.

looked over-styled and ugly next to crisp-looking new cars like the Austin 1100. It was an over-reaction to the dying days of outrageous car design typified by the 1959 Cadillac Deville with its towering rear fins and larded-on chrome; but on a Dagenham scale. More than that, it was actually the design work of one Roy Brown, the man who had penned Ford's ill-fated Edsel.

There were two- and four-door versions, and the Consul Classic also spawned a coupé, the Consul Capri. With its cut-down roof and pillarless construction, this at least brought a touch of Beverly Hills glamour to Bolton and Barnsley, and is a rare beast today.

The Consul Classic sold poorly for three years before the Cortina's huge success (the two cars shared only the Classic's later 1.5-litre engine) rendered it a rare blot on Ford's customer-led copy book.

The Ford Film Unit's staff debate the Classic's finer points as they shoot *Classic Holiday*, a promotional film for the trendy new family saloon.

## ON THE PLUS SIDE

You've got to hand it to Ford: they took a risk and tried to give the poor old British driver a taste of motoring life on the other side of the Pond, without the fuel consumption the British Treasury would render unacceptable. The Consul Classic today has charm by the bucket-load.

# AMERICA'S LIVELY PONY THAT BECAME LEE'S THRIFTY GELDING

The Ford Mustang is one of the most successful motoring constructs of all time: it was the original 'Personal Car', a (relatively) compact two-plus-two that used straightforward mechanical units in a sporty-ish package. Neither pure roadster nor sensible coupe, the Mustang fitted the bill perfectly for many suburban Americans. In its first year of production, 1964, 418,000 were sold, and the series topped 1m in 1969.

Ford's high-powered adventures with the GT350 version – the car Steve McQueen took to a cool new pinnacle in movie car chases in *Bullitt* – turned the Mustang into a true muscle car in the early 1970s. But in 1973, Ford boss Lee Iacocca shocked and dismayed the Mustang fraternity with the Mustang II.

With a fuel crisis impending, it was depressingly appropriate, 20in shorter than the outgoing Mustangs, 500lb lighter, and sharing many parts with Ford's horrible Pinto economy car – a vehicle with a propensity for catching fire. For the first time, there was no convertible version, while the basic engine was an unlovely 2.3-litre four-cylinder.

Of course, its truncated size made it much more suitable for English roads than its forebears, but the obligatory left-hand drive was a major off-put for UK buyers who might have been tempted otherwise. Still, a 5-litre

Best Selling

RATED **3rd** OUT OF **10**

Sold: 1,107,718

No bigger than a Capri but not much fun to drive, the Mustang II was designed for recession-hit American singletons; this is a UK-registered example.

V8 engine option added the right noises, if not that much extra urge.

The Mustang II, of course, helped Ford get through a trying time for American car makers; the mid-1970s saw the environmental, consumer and economical screws turned hard on Detroit's thumbs. But its crisply styled replacement, the Mustang III, couldn't come a moment too soon.

### ON THE PLUS SIDE

Even the relatively small original Mustang was a big car by British standards, particularly one designed for a single man- or girl-about-town. The Mustang II has some of the flavour of the first models in a package about the size of Ford's European 'personal' car – the Capri.

That's more like it: the original 1964 Ford Mustang was immensely popular, especially in V8 form when it became one of the first American 'muscle' cars.

The fastback version of the Mustang II, in this case a sporty Mach I. In this format, its close relationship to the awful Pinto is obvious.

# THE HILLMAN 'HARD-UP' HUSKY: A MONGREL FOR THE MASSES

When it came to making customers feel bad about being poor, British car manufacturers of the post-war period had a special knack. The Hillman Husky was a good example of their austerity specials, a stripped-out model for the 'this-is-all-you-get' stratum of cash-strapped buyer. The Rootes Group tried it first in 1954 when it created the Husky concept by putting some windows and a back seat into a Hillman Minx-derived Commer Cob van and re-christening it.

This stumpy little affair did well despite an absolute purge on creature comforts – even a heater was an extra. So a new Husky was planned for the arrival of the sleek new 1956

The first Hillman Husky destined, Rootes claimed, for 'the estate owner, farmer, small-holder, one-man business, the camper, the sportsman or the family man'.

This was what they wanted: Husky buyers were willing to forsake creature comforts for versatility and this useful chunk of cargo space.

**ON THE PLUS SIDE**

Cars like the Hillman Husky made our parents' world go round: highly practical with van-like rear doors, useful, reliable, trusty. It was the sort of boxy runabout that was ideal for people starting a business, or even ferrying the family and all its paraphernalia around at a miserly cost.

Minx generation. Except, it came two years later, leaving the dumpy old model to soldier on and make its owners feel even more second-rate.

Once again, the new one was simply a delivery van with windows in the sides and a folding back seat – retaining its two, side-opening rear doors – and all unnecessary frills were shorn off it.

You could say it pre-dated today's practical and comfortable runabouts like the Citroën Berlingo. Except this was Hillman in the 1950s and '60s, which meant ruggedness taking precedence over refinement.

The old Minx series was pensioned off in the mid-1960s but the Husky name resurfaced in 1967 on a rudely cubic estate version of the Hillman Imp. Once again, this was really a Commer Imp van with windows, but this time it was a compromised load-lugger because its rear-mounted engine was under the floor. It was a predictable flop and is, nowadays, rare.

*Don't be fooled by the two-tone paintwork and the whitewall tyres – the Husky, in second generation form here, was a strictly utilitarian affair.*

## THE HILLMAN IMP
### AT A GLANCE

**Built**: 1963–76 in Linwood, Glasgow
**Engine**: four-cylinder, 875cc
**Top speed**: 90mph
**Price when new**: £508
**Number produced**: 440,032

### ON THE MINUS SIDE

There are lots of things to blame for the Imp's failure: the poor design, the high price, the recalcitrant Scottish workforce. They all added up to a car that was unreliable and unnecessarily odd. The Imp never sold well and it lost Rootes/Chrysler (and the British government) a sackful of money.

# WHAT DID FOR THE IMP? BEETLE THINKING AND THE 'RED JOCKS'

Britain's small cars of the 1950s were almost uniformly dreary but in 1959 the Mini, Anglia and Herald broke new ground. The Rootes Group – makers of Hillmans, Humbers, Singers and Sunbeams – was without a small car in its arsenal for another four years.

And when it came in 1963 it, too, was very different, Sadly, for all the wrong reasons. The Mini was proving front-wheel drive was the way ahead for tiny, roomy cars but Rootes turned instead to the VW Beetle-like ruse of putting the engine in the back.

That allowed decent cabin space but also made for tail-heavy weight distribution.

Rootes wanted to build the Imp in Coventry but government planners had other ideas: they agreed to lend money to the company only if a new factory was erected in economically depressed – but staunchly militant – Glasgow.

Technically, the Hillman Imp was intriguing. The 875cc engine was a light-alloy overhead camshaft unit derived from a Coventry Climax racing engine. That made it nippy and versatile, and tuned Imps were very successful on the track. Rootes offered its own tuned 50bhp engine in versions called Sunbeam Imp Sport and, with a fastback roof, Sunbeam Stiletto. Other Imp derivatives were the fastback Imp Californian, up-market Super Imp, Commer van, Husky estate and plush Singer Chamois.

### ON THE PLUS SIDE

People who bought Imps and ironed out their irksome problems grew to love them – from the elderly lady using hers as a shopping trolley to the deft racing driver (a well-sorted Imp can be a surprisingly rapid and nimble mover) who knew the Imp could be a giant-killer in the right, if skilled, hands.

The square-rigged face of the 1963 Hillman Imp was in stark contrast to the rounded profile of the Mini, and its engine was at the opposite end too.

Sadly the Imp gained a reputation for unreliability. Its quirky pneumatic throttle was troublesome and was quickly changed; Imps further suffered from water leaks, gasket failures and overheating engines. Plus, the Imp cost more than a Mini, was sparsely trimmed and less well packaged. The practical lifting rear window and folding rear seats were small recompense.

The Imp was a sort of half-way hatchback, with this handy opening rear window and folding seats inside to make a trip to Fine Fare a doddle.

## Daftest Features

RATED **3rd** OUT OF **10**

Engine in the back like a Beetle but without VW's high quality

A wide variety of Imp models included this Singer Chamois Sport with four headlamps, a more luxurious cabin and those natty wheeltrims.

She might have been filming Carry On Doctor and about to start a UK tour with Engelbert Humperdinck, but in 1965 Anita Harris chose a Sunbeam Stiletto, poor girl.

## Best Selling

RATED **10th** OUT OF **10**

Sold: 440,032

**Built**: 1967–76 in Ryton on Dunsmore, West Midlands and Linwood, Glasgow

**Engine**: four-cylinder, 1725cc

**Top speed**: 98mph

**Price when new**: £1.138

**Number produced**: 43,951

### ON THE MINUS SIDE

Pretentious, pretentious, pretentious: the Sceptre was the Hyacinth Bucket of the car world, all chintzy curtains and neighbour-rattling prestige. It was just as tedious as the Hillman Hunter to drive, and there wasn't even leather upholstery as a nostalgic (and worth having) throwback to the good old Humber days.

# A LITTLE BIT OF SNOB APPEAL FOR OUR SCEPTRED SUBURBS

I could, patient readers, fill this book with examples of 'badge engineering'. This dubious motor industry practice is deceptively simple: you make one basic car and then, to sell as many as possible through several outlets with the minimum of effort, you apply a variety of different badges, nameplates and finishes to it.

You do not make any engineering changes, either mechanical or metalwork ones, to it to differentiate these cars – that could result in costly design re-appraisal. Then you sit back and watch the punters lap up your marketing strategy.

Surprisingly, maybe, Rolls-Royce began the identikit practice in 1949 with the all-but-identical Bentley Mk VI and Rolls Silver Dawn, and the British Motor Corporation and the Rootes Group joined it with the 1957 Riley 1.5/Wolseley 1500 and 1958 Hillman Minx/Singer Gazelle respectively.

By the time the tarted-up Hillman Hunter you see here came along for Humber agents to peddle, the practice was widespread – even Jaguar made doppelgangers (Daimler Sovereign/Jag 420). Worse, there were Singer and, for export, Sunbeam editions too.

Customers might have been dim-witted but they weren't going to be conned into paying a huge premium for four headlights and a vinyl roof. Rootes merely did a comprehensive job of reducing formerly prestigious or sporty brands to worthlessness. Moreover, it was fiddling while Rome burnt: it concentrated on petty marque differences rather than making one really good basic design.

So was the Humber Sceptre, with its overdrive, fancy wheeltrims and – yes – twin reversing lamps – really such a bad car? Well, possibly not the worst, but it's not a car you'd cross the road to drool over, is it?

The Humber Sceptre was simply a fancy, 'badge-engineered' version of the Hillman Hunter, and traded on Humber's

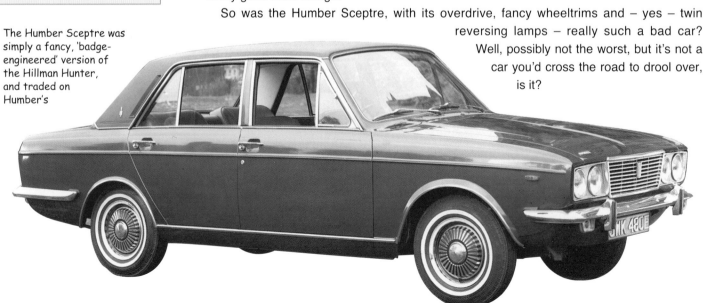

For the last two years of the Sceptre's – and Humber's – existence, there was also an estate, with a built-in roof rack among its standard kit.

## ON THE PLUS SIDE

The Hunter ain't no dog – after all, they've been making them under licence in Iran for 25 years, and it's that beleaguered nation's pride and joy because it's robust and reliable. Add in a few creature comforts and a bit of olde-worlde Humber kudos and for many it's the perfect motor car.

The Peykan has been Iran's 'national car' for 25 years – essentially a mildly updated version of the Hunter/Sceptre, it's long past its prime.

**Built:** 1974–83, in Seoul, South Korea

**Engine:** four-cylinder, 1238/1439cc

**Top speed:** 91mph (1.4-litre)

**Price when new:** £3,296 (1.2-litre three-door)

**Number produced:** 361,432 (including some locally assembled Fords)

# HUMDRUM AFFAIR THAT GAVE A GLITTERING KOREA TO HYUNDAI

*Designed, would you believe, by Giorgetto Giugiaro, the Hyundai Pony was South Korea's first indigenous car design, with British and Japanese know-how.*

If you've bought a Korean-made car, chances are you're pretty happy with it. They may not be especially exciting but the buyers keep on coming. They may not be as exacting as the Japanese car makers, but Korean manufacturers know that happy customers are ones who don't need to return to the showroom holding bits that have snapped off.

It's easy to forget Korea built its first home-conceived car only 27 years ago. And here it is in all its glory – the Hyundai Pony.

True, it's not exactly a car you'd make a detour to ogle. It possesses the visual charm of a tinny mid-1970s Datsun crossed with a Morris Marina – although the styling, amazingly, was by that usually inspired Italian Giorgio Giugiaro.

The three-door Pony looked uncannily like a Morris Marina coupé; it was a reliable runabout but the last car in the world you'd get excited about.

## ON THE MINUS SIDE

Like those TV shows about the early lives of film stars, the first Pony is not a car Hyundai would want to brag about today. You'd never guess it had Italian styling, while the Mitsubishi engines and assorted British bits don't set the pulse racing either. As they say: 'They all had to start somewhere'.

## ON THE PLUS SIDE

Hyundai took the bold step of creating its own car, albeit with some assistance from experienced outsiders, and not simply bolting together someone else's redundo products. With the neat and reliable Pony, they proved they were up to the mark on the quality front too. As they say: 'The rest is history'.

Engines and other mechanical bits were provided by Mitsubishi, while most of the expertise involved in building the factory and showing Koreans how to actually make cars came from Britain, orchestrated by an ex-British Leyland executive called George Turnbull.

How his colleagues in the West Midlands might have jeered when he headed east, but just look at what Turnbull started; even though its wannabe rival Daewoo hit the skids, Hyundai has joined the world car industry's big guns.

It now boasts, for example, the best-selling coupé in Italy, as well as having swallowed up another Korean brand, Kia, and entered the off-roader market with the Santa Fe. But you will search for excitement in the first Pony in vain: it is, quite possibly, one of the most thoroughly uninspiring motor cars of all time . . . and it didn't come to the UK until it was seven years old.

The full range of first-generation Ponys included a useful pick-up, which made it to the UK market, and an estate, which didn't.

## THE INVICTA BLACK PRINCE

AT A GLANCE

**Built**: 1946–50, in Virginia Water, Surrey
**Engine**: six-cylinder, 2998cc
**Top speed**: unknown
**Price when new**: £3,579 (Wentworth saloon)
**Number produced**: 16

Worst Selling
RATED **4th** OUT OF **10**
Number Sold: 16

# ATTEMPT TO UNSEAT ROLLS WAS TOO CLEVER FOR ITS OWN GOOD

The end of the Second World War brought a flurry of attempts to cash in on the huge, pent-up demand for new cars. Some, like Healey and Bristol, achieved immortality in the minds of car enthusiasts. The Invicta Black Prince, however, was too complex by half, and made a brief splash before vanishing into obscurity.

An enormous luxury car newly designed from stem to stern, the Black Prince used an all-aluminium Meadows six-cylinder, 3-litre engine with triple carburettors and two sparkplugs per cylinder. Its power was transmitted through a complex version of today's constantly variable automatic transmissions. Called a 'Brockhouse Hydro-Kinetic Turbo Transmitter', it did away with a conventional gearbox altogether.

### ON THE MINUS SIDE

When you take on the big guns you must make sure you have the firepower to confront them. The Black Prince, despite a noble background and a fantastic on-paper specification, was simply too complicated and under-funded to ever have been successful; grand folly is how it seems in retrospect.

No question, the Invicta Black Prince was a handsome machine, but its complexity meant it would never rival Rolls-Royce and Lagonda.

The car came from the drawing board of William Watson, designer of the wonderful 1930s Invictas like the 4.5-litre and S-type. He was responsible for the advanced chassis with its all-round torsion bar suspension, 24-volt starter and electrics with trickle charging, and built-in electric jacks. The radiator had its own immersion heater to prevent freezing.

The bodies, saloons, convertibles and even an estate, were made by outside coachbuilders on a special vibration-free floorpan, mounted with rubber bushes to the chassis.

It was a sumptuous object but at almost £4,000 by 1949, a Black Prince cost 10 times the price of a typical small family saloon like a Ford Popular – putting it well beyond even the most successful 1940s black marketeers.

The project began amid much fanfare in 1946 but owing to the colossal price, the post-war scarcity of raw materials, and myriad problems of getting so much new technology to function harmoniously, it folded in 1950, and little more was heard of it.

The faulty transmission reputedly rendered the car almost impossible to use. Still, an incredible 12 of the 16 cars actually completed survive.

Most Unreliable

RATED **4th** OUT OF **10**

An advanced car that jammed itself into reverse

## ON THE PLUS SIDE

The Black Prince was a magnificent – and thoroughbred – attempt to match the best in the world with a British super-saloon. Who knows how effective it could have been with the right backing and a little bit of faith from those sour doubting Thomases of the unforgiving post-war period?

This is the Wentworth saloon, but every Invicta Black Prince had individually made coachwork: they were all fearfully expensive.

## THE JAGUAR 2.4-LITRE MKI

### AT A GLANCE

**Built**: 1955–59 in Coventry, West Midlands

**Engine**: six-cylinder, 2483cc

**Top speed**: 102mph

**Price when new**: £1,344

**Number produced**: 19,400

### ON THE MINUS SIDE

Slab-sided little number that was gutless and rust-prone – not a description you'd normally attach to a Jag but sadly appropriate here. And when Jag added more power for the Mk1 3.4, it created a wayward beast with handling that was seriously at odds with its electric acceleration.

It may not have the speed of other Jaguar saloons, but the monocoque-construction 2.4 still has all the glamour and image that define the marque.

# UNDERPOWERED SLUG HARDLY DOES JAGUAR NAME JUSTICE

The Jaguar MkII is, for many, the absolute essence of a classic British sports saloon, with its gorgeous lines, firecracker performance and acres of wood-and-leather character.

The MkI, however, has never been held in such high esteem.

Its looks, with stingy, pillbox-like windows, a heavily domed roof and rear wheels concealed behind long metal 'spats', were tidy but slab-sided.

And, while you could get an acceptable 27mpg if you drove it extremely gingerly, the 2.4-litre version of the classic Jaguar twin-cam engine, the smallest ever, hardly endowed

the MkI – or simply '2.4-litre saloon' as it was officially termed when it was revealed in 1955 – with lightning acceleration. With automatic transmission, this cat's claws were clipped still further. The interior was, at least, well up to classy Jaguar standards.

In 1955, when the MkI was launched, it was a Jaguar milestone because it was the first to get rid of the old-fashioned separate chassis in favour of fully unitary construction. Sadly, Jaguar's inexperience with making cars this way also resulted in the MkI rotting with the speed of last year's compost.

A power hike came with the 3.4-litre in 1957 but this, conversely, was overpowered for its narrow rear track and weedy drum brakes. The 1959 MkII was, everyone recognises today, a huge improvement on just about every front, with disc brakes, vastly improved handling and a styling makeover that turned it from ugly duckling to understated darling.

Still, the few MkIs surviving make splendid period pieces. And it was, after all, the car from which the modern Jaguar – albeit hesitatingly – leapt.

*Not especially fast and, some say, a bit slab-sided, the 2.4-litre brought the Jaguar ownership experience to a much wider audience.*

### ON THE PLUS SIDE

Much of the fun of a Jaguar is in its sheer glamour, and the smooth-looking Mk1 has 1950s style in spades. If you fancy a period classic that pushes all the right sensory buttons but won't break the bank to run then this could be the underrated bargain you've been looking for.

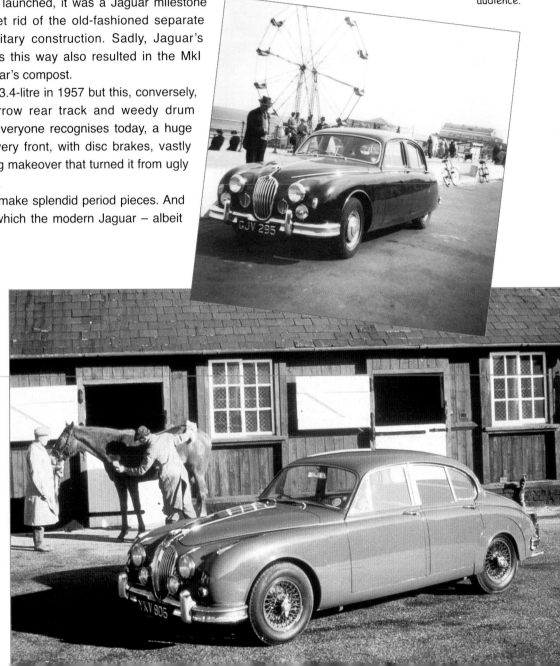

*In 1959 came the Jaguar MkII, which cured most of the problems of the earlier models – including the MkI 3.4-litre's alarming handling.*

**Built**: 1972–76 in West Bromwich, West Midlands
**Engine**: four-cylinder, 1973cc
**Top speed**: 120mph
**Price when new**: £1,810
**Number produced**: 10,926

## ON THE MINUS SIDE

Believe it or not, this unconvincing cocktail of motoring ideas was supposed to be a spiritual replacement for the much-loved Austin-Healey 3000. An ill-judged concept, however, turned into a nightmare of quality problems for trusting buyers. Few cars of the early 1970s made a TR6 seem high quality . . . but this was one of them.

# THE RIGHT INGREDIENTS BUT THIS HEALEY WAS HALF-BAKED

What a great little roadster the Jensen-Healey should have been. Built – in metal – by Jensen, designed and refined by Donald Healey, powered by a reliable Vauxhall engine, capable of 120mph and 25mpg, aimed at the lucrative US market – this was to be a British sports car in the best traditions. Critics of the time praised its performance and road manners. So what went wrong?

Well, first there was the design. From a pleasingly simple and sleek initial shape by designer Hugo Poole, the Jensen-Healey became bland and, with its thick, US-style rubber bumpers, a bit cack-handed. Jensen owner Kjell Qvale knew it must meet American safety rules, but there had to be a neater way of achieving it.

The left-hand drive is the clue to the Jensen-Healey's intended role – a replacement for the Austin-Healey 3000, a very popular British export to the US.

The Jensen-Healey sporting its optional hardtop; it was quite a clean design rather spoilt by ham-fisted detail design to meet American safety laws.

## ON THE PLUS SIDE

The Jensen-Healey is a fun car to drive and, with a well-sorted, well-maintained engine, should give years of entertainment. Its demise was as much to do with external factors as design compromises, and on a day-to-day basis, it offers rather more sophistication and comfort than your regular MGs and Triumphs.

And then, the engine: Qvale was persuaded by Lotus boss Colin Chapman to substitute the dependable GM lump for his new and largely untried Lotus 2-litre twin-cam unit.

It should have given sparkling performance. Instead, the engine had numerous teething problems that meant early Jensen-Healey owners spent more time in the back of taxis than at the wheel of their new sports cars.

Then, a few years on, the cars started to rust. Badly. The economic recession of the time was another good reason to steer clear of a strife-ridden new sports car.

The Jensen-Healey's woes were not helped by atrocious industrial relations between Qvale and his Jensen workforce, with consequently patchy build quality. By the time the San Francisco-based sports car tycoon decided to put the company into receivership in 1976, customers for the Jensen-Healey – and its sports-estate derivative the Jensen GT – were few and far between.

**Fastest**

RATED **6th** OUT OF **10**

Max speed: 120 mph

**Most Unreliable**

RATED **5th** OUT OF **10**

Lotus engine is a dream, when it works properly

J attrill '72

Under the metal skin, the Jensen-Healey used many Vauxhall parts but – crucially – not the engine, which was a temperamental Lotus unit.

## THE KIA PRIDE
### AT A GLANCE

**Built**: 1991–2000 in Asan Bay, South Korea
**Engine**: four-cylinder, 1139/1324cc
**Top speed**: 91mph
**Price when new**: £5,799
**Number produced**: unknown

### ON THE MINUS SIDE

The Pride was a trap for the uninformed buyer: it purported to be a new model when it had already led a previous life as a Mazda. The canny used car trade, however, ruthlessly ranked it as low-priced forecourt fodder when it came to trade-in time, to the dismay of proud owners.

# KIA WAS PROUD OF IT, EVEN IF EVERYONE ELSE WAS UNIMPRESSED

You shouldn't speak ill of the dead, and the Kia Pride is still warm in its grave. Yet this is a car which, in its brand-new guise, died the first time a full 10 years ago. As the Mazda 121, it had a three-year life between 1988 and 1991 before – we thought – being consigned to history.

When we first glimpsed the 121, we noted its tall, upright design – making it perfect for arthritis-ridden older relations to potter down to the shops in. But that was about all that was interesting: the rest of the car was conventional and mundane.

In fact, the 121 was never a Mazda pure and simple. It was conceived by the Japanese company in association with Ford as a cut-price commuter car aimed at the rock-bottom end of the US market, where it was marketed as the Ford Festiva. To this end, production was farmed out to a Korean motoring sweatshop no-one had heard of: Kia.

However, when Mazda decided to stop selling its version, Kia was allowed to take the design over, and used it as a leg-up to becoming a car maker proper.

Hence the Pride's appearance in Britain in 1991, in three- and five-door formats, as a bargain-basement runabout, forming a launchpad for Kia's own cars. Desperate for something, anything, to get us to notice it, Kia re-introduced us to whitewall tyres on the Pride. And that was it as far as innovations went.

The Pride remained on sale here for the rest of the decade, only vanishing after the company was swallowed up by Hyundai and this ageing motoring embarrassment was finally expunged.

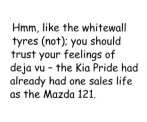

Hmm, like the whitewall tyres (not); you should trust your feelings of deja vu – the Kia Pride had already had one sales life as the Mazda 121.

Hard to fault the Kia Pride as a cheap family runabout, really, but there was nothing sparkling in the way it performed its daily duties.

No-one had heard of Kia until it gained the rights to the Ford Festiva; since then, the firm's burgeoning output has flooded out of its Asan Bay factory.

## ON THE PLUS SIDE

There really is very little wrong with the Pride if you just require a runabout for trundling, urban errands. The Mazda design is safe and sound, and the all-round economy and ease of driving should easily outweigh any deficiencies in the driving excitement department. Plus, check out those sassy whitewalls. . . .

## THE LADA SAMARA
### AT A GLANCE

**Built**: 1984 to today in Togliatti, Russia
**Engine**: four-cylinder, 1089/1288/1499cc
**Top speed**: 97mph
**Price when new**: £4,595
**Number produced**: unknown

# 'LADA YOU THAN ME', THAT WAS YOUR CATCHPHRASE

Lada has been a whipping boy for Soviet Bloc motors for a quarter of a century and, as far as its early cars are concerned – the 1200s, 1500s and later Rivas – it's a touch unfair.

Designed from scratch with help from Porsche, the three- and five-door Samaras were still miles behind their European rivals in refinement terms.

Heavily subsidised by the Russian state (they'd have been hopelessly uncompetitive otherwise), these Fiat 124 lookalikes with their Moskvich-derived engines were tough as nails. For someone who had to have a spanking new car sitting on the drive, a Lada made sense, no matter how primitive it soon was.

But then Lada decided to go it alone, and design its own cars. With no experience, it called on Porsche to help come up with a new car, new engine and new front-wheel drive drivetrain. This was a big undertaking and, all things considered, the 1984 Samara looked a sterling effort.

To drive or touch it, however, was another matter entirely – merely looking like a passable Escort alternative was not enough. The Samara, initially a three- or five-door although later a four-door saloon joined them, was a dull drive, with below-par refinement and a bouncy ride more suited to getting through Moscow's appalling streets than along Maidenhead's (comparatively) silky-smooth high street.

The slipshod fit and finish of the cheap plastic trim inside added to the third-rate image, and it's worth pointing out that almost every Lada sold in the UK was virtually rebuilt in a factory in North Humberside – sometimes including a total respray – before it was fit to greet its new owner.

In the end, it was the Samara's inability to meet Europe's stringent exhaust emission rules that saw its departure from British showrooms.

Hardly a thrill to drive, the Samara was a downward rollercoaster ride all the way in the value stakes, as crippling depreciation took its toll.

Rows of Lada Samaras receiving major cosmetic surgery at a Bridlington plant to make them saleable – quality of factory-fresh cars was always appalling.

## ON THE PLUS SIDE

Any motor car designed for life in Russia is going to have to be rugged, and the Samara (and other Lada models), while a bit rough and ready, will take a hammering in everyday use. If that sort of stamina is important, then a Samara would beat a Maestro, a Tipo or a BX hands down.

## ON THE MINUS SIDE

It didn't matter how often motoring pundits implored their readers to buy a good secondhand car rather than a new Lada, certain buyers would countenance nothing else. They even ignored warnings about the catastrophic depreciation these clunkers enjoyed . . . although rest assured they paid the price for that when trying to sell them.

The car that started it all: here is one of the very first Ladas, outwardly identical to the Fiat 124 on which it was based, pictured in 1974.

**Built**: 1979–81 in Chivasso, Italy and Milton Keynes, Buckinghamshire
**Engine**: four-cylinder, 1995cc
**Top speed**: 117mph
**Price when new**: £6,187
**Number produced**: 300

### ON THE MINUS SIDE

This was a truly desperate attempt by Lancia to shift its metal – metal which had, in some cases, started to corrode even before cars reached the showroom. Stickers and fancy radios were insufficient to mask such a fundamental failing, and this cheesy limited-edition helped hasten Lancia's UK demise, not stem it.

Fastest
RATED **7th** OUT OF **10**

Max speed:
117 mph

Spoilers, stripes, fancy wheels, sunroof and a decent stereo were all part of the Coupé Hi-Fi package, all thanks to Aston Martin's magic-makers.

# HMM, LOVELY STRIPES: ARE THEY ACTUALLY HOLDING IT TOGETHER?

In the late 1970s, Lancias had quite a spectacular reputation in Britain – for rusting. Tales of engines breaking off corroded mountings, and brand new paintwork pitted with brown marks, were legion.

Once favoured as an Italian BMW much admired by the chic middle classes, Lancias turned into undesirable backstreet bangers when just a couple of years old. In 1993, the marque disappeared from Britain altogether after a last-ditch push to interest us in the Dedra and Thema, decent cars both by then.

The Beta Coupé Hi-Fi was born in the eye of this disastrous public relations storm. In 1981, there were rows of unsold Beta Coupés on windswept airfields so the importer asked Aston Martin to help shift them. This was at a time when the great British sports car company was setting up its own contract engineering offshoot – aping its rival Porsche – and so this Lancia rescue job formed a cornerstone of its new Tickford division

Aston kitted 300 of the cleaned-up and heavily rust-proofed cars out with alloy wheels and low-profile tyres, a rear spoiler and front air-dam, and snazzy side stripes.

Only 300 people will ever own a specification like this.

And, of course, a decent hi-fi – a Voxson Indianapolis with graphic equaliser, four speakers and an electric aerial. No CD autochanger, this, but smart for then.

Unfortunately, though, the damage was done and the Hi-Fi did little to halt Lancia's disastrous sales slump – especially as the specialist press got wind of the fact that the cars had been lying around unsold for up to two years. Still, the stereo did at least help drown out the usual Beta squeaks and rattles.

### ON THE PLUS SIDE

No-one likes a rotter – and some Lancias represent pears in this respect – but the Coupé Hi-Fi was thoroughly (if belatedly) rust-proofed, and was always a joy to drive with its responsive engine and sparkling handling. So no arguing with engine or stereo notes, but how many survived?

Lancia might have found 300 mugs to buy its tarted-up rot-boxes, but the Beta Coupé Hi-Fi was a desperate attempt to rescue its damaged reputation.

And this is what the car should have looked like – a standard Lancia Beta Coupé 2000; terrible reputation for rust killed the marque in Britain.

**Built**: 1960 in Coventry, West Midlands
**Engine**: six-cylinder, 2553cc
**Top speed**: unknown
**Price when new**: £2,096
**Number produced**: 3

Ugliest
RATED **3rd** OUT OF **10**

Two cigars and a circulargrilledonota fine car make

# TWO CIGARS, LILAC PAINT AND A LIBERAL SPRINKLING OF GOLD DUST

'The pulsating car of the moment – and of the future' in 1960. Never was an advertising epithet so misplaced. With car manufacture fizzled out by the late 1950s, the old-established Lea-Francis company, based in Coventry, was losing money hand over fist when its biggest shareholder stepped in as chairman.

A building contractor, Kenneth Benfield knew zip about making cars. But he knew what he liked.

He'd seen magazine pictures of the latest Italian super cars – particularly show cars designed by Ghia – and, thus inspired, he ordered his beleaguered staff to cobble together a sports car to revive Lea-Francis, using a Ford Zephyr six-cylinder engine for power. The chassis was a tubular affair, and boasted disc brakes on all four wheels.

The firm's PR man, also a part-time cartoonist and stand-up comedian, was drafted in as unwilling stylist. 'Benfield wanted two cigars in a catamaran with a round radiator,' recalled one insider.

To make it even more up-to-the-minute, the 1960 'Lynx' motor show car was painted lilac with gold-plated trim, but the catchy ads, and even a cover appearance on *Vanity Fair* magazine couldn't stem the showgoers' scornful laughter at the £2,096 monster.

Lea-Francis was so hard up it couldn't afford to make any production cars unless they were actually ordered. And as none were, the Lynx sloped

Helen Pae, aged 18, examines the Lynx's three carburettors at the 1960 Earl's Court motor show – the ill-fated car's first and last public outing.

off quietly into obscurity and L-F gave up on car manufacture completely. Further revivals have been mooted and even attempted since, although the Jaguar-powered 'replicar' Ace of Spades, theoretically on sale since the mid-1980s, is, if anything, even worse looking than the Lynx, albeit beautifully constructed.

## ON THE MINUS SIDE

At the time the lilac-painted Lynx made its only show appearance at Earl's Court in 1960s, the quality Lea-Francis image was already a distant memory. This ghastly concoction of pirated styling ideas and borrowed components did nothing to halt that, and Lea-Francis revivals have been thwarted ever since.

## ON THE PLUS SIDE

Tricky one to defend, this. If you have a perverse liking for heroic failures then the Lynx appeals for its sheer folly value alone. With a different approach in 1960, Mr Benjafield's Lea-Francis could today be a Jaguar rival . . . but, then, I couldn't have had the pleasure of including it in this book.

RATED **Worst 2nd** OUT OF **10**

Number sold: 3

Believe me, this is the most flattering view of the Lynx, whose lines were drawn by a cartoonist to the tastes of a West Midlands builder.

The Lea-Francis Ace of Spades was an uncomfortable amalgam of styles but, none the less, it's kept the Lea-Francis marque alive for some 20 years.

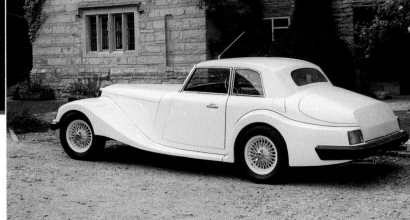

# LLOYD PROVED THAT GRIMSBY WASN'T ON THE MOTORING MAP

Often hailed as a trail-blazing precursor to the Mini, the Lloyd 650 was a bad car. Fascinating, but terrible. Roland Lloyd, car-mad son of a wealthy Grimsby fish merchant, yearned to build his own 'working man's car'. His Lloyd 350 had a two-stroke motorbike engine and a tiny two-seater body. Between 1935 and 1940, he sold 300.

Buoyed by military contract work, he set a more ambitious target after the Second World War.

He wanted to incorporate front-wheel drive and a transversely-mounted engine, just as Alec Issigonis chose to for the 1959 Mini, in a 'light car'. He designed and built his own aluminium, two-stroke, 654cc engine, a backbone chassis, independent coil-spring suspension, and precise rack and pinion steering.

The body was a surprisingly attractive four-seater tourer, panelled in aluminium, and the car was unveiled at a 1946 Cleethorpes trade fair. The press liked its nimbleness and cars started to trickle off the production line in 1948, mostly destined for foreign owners in those export-or-die times.

But under the surface, it was all going wrong. Endless design and manufacturing problems meant production was slow and warranty claims high. Customers eventually lost patience, and the initial target of

Roland Lloyd sitting in one of the prototypes of his Lloyd 650; an insistence on making almost every part of the car himself led to the company's downfall.

### ON THE MINUS SIDE

Just 10 Lloyd 650s remain: few are roadworthy although Jim Blezard of Preston, Lancashire spent an amazing 10 years renovating one. In the process, he virtually wrote the instruction manual because, when they were new, few 650s ever lasted long enough for shared knowledge of them to be passed on.

five a week was achieved just once. Price was also a stumbling block. A Ford Anglia was £150 cheaper.

Dwindling cashflow halted production by 1951, after fewer than 400 had been built. For those who had bought Roland Lloyd's brave creation, this was grim news. But the company's creditors saved the company by insisting car production was abandoned in favour of general engineering.

The 650 was an attractive little car, sharing many design features with two-stroke contemporaries from continental Europe, such as Germany's DKW.

**Most Unreliable**

RATED **6th** OUT OF **10**

Made totally in Grimsby, that centre of engineering excellence (not)

The Lloyd 650 was launched at a trade fair in Cleethorpes in 1946, the seaside resort adjoining the fishing port of Grimsby, home to the Lloyd factory.

# AUSTRALIA'S 'VOLVO ESTATE' WAS A CUT-PRICE UK FLOP

You might confidently expect a big saloon or estate with a 2.6-litre engine to boast six-cylinder smoothness, but not the Lonsdale. When it went on sale in the UK in 1983, the range-topping 2.6-litre edition actually featured the biggest four-cylinder engine then on sale here – bigger even than the Lancia Gamma's barmy 2.5-litre four.

Adding to the gutless wonder image, the car generated just 102bhp, and most came with a Borg Warner four-speed automatic gearbox.

But what exactly is a Lonsdale, I hear you ask. Well, just take a look at it. That's right, everything says Mitsubishi Sigma and the car shares much with this undistinguished Japanese family saloon. The Lonsdale, however, was built in Australia – hence, with its right-hand drive, the ease with which it could be sold here – in a factory once owned by Chrysler.

The basic design was indeed Japanese, but that big old engine, euphemistically called the 'Astron', was an all-Australian confection (although 1.6s and 2-litres were offered too),

Two-tone paint and alloy wheels cheer up the ageing looks of the Lonsdale 2.6 as the limited-run Satellite (above); unadorned (right) it's a dead-ringer for a Mitsubishi Galant.

and these cars, tough and simple with their live rear axles, were popular in the Outback.

Called Lonsdales only for the UK, however, they cut an unsophisticated dash, and the Colt Car Company, the British importer who also brought us Japanese Mitsubishis, soon wished it had never embarked on this unprofitable sideline. In just 13 months on sale, a mere few hundred Lonsdales – most of them estates – were sold. Bar a handful of over-powered Holden saloons imported in the last few years, the Lonsdale was the last Australian car to be sold in Britain.

### ON THE PLUS SIDE

Let's face it, not every antique dealer, horsebox tow-er and small shopkeeper could afford a Volvo estate, no matter how much they might have wanted one. The Lonsdale estate, therefore, offered sturdiness and practicality for far fewer (Australian) dollars. They don't make 'em this simple any more.

Here is the car the Lonsdale was based on, the Mitsubishi Galant – in this case, a turbocharged 1983 model which could reach a rather unnerving 127mph.

Fastest
RATED **8th** OUT OF **10**
Max speed: 111 mph

The Lonsdale estate, especially with the ex-Chrysler 2.6-litre engine, was a gutsy, cut-price Volvo alternative – despite just four cylinders.

# PSST; WANNA BUY A REAL PIECE OF MOTORING HISTORY?

Think of the manufacture of reproduction antiques and you'll probably picture a couple of villains churning out replica Hepplewhite chairs from unseasoned pine. Quite probably, you won't think of a bustling Indian factory bolting together four-wheel drive vehicles.

But that's what happens in Bombay, where Mahindra & Mahindra have been building Jeeps under licence since 1954. It's made close to half a million of them, including 30,000 for the Iranian army, and continues to do so in spite of finding a big seller in the Ford Escort, which it has constructed under licence since 1997.

The stripes and sporty seats don't even start to disguise the Mahindra's 1954 Jeep origins. This model was marketed, appropriately, as the 'Indian Brave'.

The thing is, while Jeep's own Jeeps have moved on in terms of comfort, refinement and performance at the same time as retaining their traditional looks, the Mahindra really is the genuine article, 1954-vintage. Okay, the diesel engines are Peugeot units and there are a few piddling design updates, but the Mahindra Jeeps are more 'authentic' than any modern Jeep model.

The Mahindra range for Britain in 1993, with the CJ5 on the left and CJ13 on the right: no doubting their ruggedness but could you take the pounding?

That means, of course, they are very, very capable off-road but also very, very crude. British imports began in 1989 but petered out in 1994 when the Mahindra – which had to be 'readied' for European buyers in a Greek factory (hmm, Indian and Greek build quality . . . nice) – could no longer keep up with EC noise and pollution demands.

At one time, the Yeovil-based importer claimed to have 100 dealers, and there was a flurry of interest in this macho-retro-chic-mobile. Customers, however, were ill-prepared for the spine-jarring ride quality, the mechanical coarseness and the abysmal build quality. Even at the low, low price, almost any other secondhand 4x4 – in virtually any condition – was preferable.

The long-wheelbase (91in) Mahindra 'Jeep' was christened the Indian Chief for us Brits, but it still utterly failed to curry favour.

The swish lines of the Biturbo Spider, launched in 1984 and with a Zagato-built body, still failed to convince Maserati aficionados.

# PATCHY BMW RIVAL LEFT TRAD MASERATI LOVERS COLD

In 1975, heavily loss-making Maserati was put into liquidation by its owner Citroën. After almost 40 years, it looked as if one of the greatest names in sports and racing cars was about to perish.

Then along came the Argentinian ex-racing driver and sometime supercar builder Alessandro de Tomaso. At the behest of an Italian governmental industrial agency, he cooked up a rescue plan and – for the princely sum of 210,000 lire (about £150), plus £3.5m in debts – he became Maserati's new owner.

Fans of the great Italian marque must have wondered what he was up to, because it was another five years before his major new Maserati, the Biturbo, was unveiled.

Where Maserati had been synonymous with sleek and sexy sports cars, however, the Biturbo was a sort of Italian BMW 3 Series, boasting a 2-litre V6 engine ably assisted by twin turbochargers, and a richly appointed interior design by Italian fashion house Missoni. Convertible and four-door versions followed, with a choice of bigger engines too.

To sports car freaks, dull but understated, and chic to its admirers, the Biturbo neverthless proved a strong seller at first. But it had some serious faults: the handling, for some, was unpredictable, but the turbochargers gave severe lag, and the reliability of electrical equipment and minor components was poor, reflecting a lax attitude to quality control in the Maserati factory.

Consequently, while the Biturbo had lots of 'showroom appeal', owners found their cars returning to the workshop all too often. British imports began in 1986 but constant changes of concessionaire meant the supply of parts and service was totally inadequate for the cars' above-average hunger for them.

The Biturbo's sumptuous interior featured fine Italian leather and woodwork, and was created by the fashion house Missoni.

Fastest

RATED **2nd** OUT OF **10**

Max speed: 132 mph

## ON THE PLUS SIDE

The Biturbo is one of the more subtly exotic cars on this planet. It's a thoroughbred example of the marque, and one which brings a wonderful engine note and entertaining handling within the grasp of the (relatively) ordinary motorist. So, it has a few faults: what Italian high-performance car doesn't?

The BMW 3 Series was the target for Alessandro de Tomaso's 'baby' Maserati; if only it had possessed BMW levels of quality and reliability.

## THE MATRA RANCHO
### AT A GLANCE

**Built:** 1977–84 in Velizy, France
**Engine:** four-cylinder, 1442cc
**Top speed:** 89mph
**Price when new:** £5,650
**Number produced:** 56,700

### ON THE MINUS SIDE

Silly plastic estate car that promised off-road ability but turned out to be nothing more than a dressed up version of a very ordinary Simca. Part of a great tradition of small French utility vehicles, the Rancho soon faded as proper 4x4s became more affordable to the wannabe country set.

# A GREAT PRETENDER THAT BEGAN A TREND FOR THE REAL THING

Are you an expert van-spotter? If so, then when you look closely at the Matra Rancho, you will instantly recognise its roots. If not, then I can reveal to you that underneath those chunky black plastic wheelarches, the jungle expedition-style spotlights and that practical, boxy rear end, is nothing more exciting than a Simca 1100 pick-up. That vehicle itself was based on the French 1967 Simca 1100, one of the first transverse-engined, front-wheel drive hatchbacks launched in Europe but generally held to be a tedious rust bucket by the mid-1970s.

The knobbly tyres, the high ground clearance, the roof rails and the guarded foglights all help hide the fact, but it's a Simca all right. Everything behind the doors, however, is Matra's own design, fashioned from glassfibre and superbly practical – later versions even featured seven seats.

A tailgate split into a glass top section and a plastic lower one meant it was versatile in a garden centre sort of way and the 1.4-litre engine, while nothing special, provided as much front-wheel driven power as most owners could want for.

The thing is, of course, that despite this rugged image the Rancho was no off-roader. It would get as stuck in shallow mud as any other family hatchback and would be no more than averagely safe in a blizzard.

It pre-dated the craze for overtly macho, four-wheel drive off-roaders; although the Range Rover had kicked this off, the 1980 Suzuki SJ had made it widely available to more impoverished but mostly urban motorists. Still, the Rancho was really little more than a roomy poseurmobile.

Matra's ingenious plastic transformation of a Simca 1100 gave Europe its first 'leisure' car, although it was definitely not an off-roader.

What it looks like in the raw – the metal front half is a Simca 1100 pick-up cab, the glassfibre back half Matra's own, boxy addition.

## ON THE PLUS SIDE

In its way, the Rancho is a design classic – a practical fun car with the overtones of outdoor activeness that have sold us on four-wheel drives. Plus, unlike its all-wheel driven peers, the Rancho is easy on petrol and simple in the engine department. Honda's 2wd HR-V is a modern-day Rancho.

Most Handy

RATED **7th** OUT OF **10**

Pioneering, roomy leisure car with low running costs

Later Ranchos could be ordered as seven-seaters, with the two extra chairs facing the rear with a good view out of the large glass tailgate.

**Built:** 1974–80 in Abingdon, Oxfordshire
**Engine:** four-cylinder, 1798cc
**Top speed:** 105mph
**Price when new:** £1,847
**Number produced:** 155,698

## ON THE MINUS SIDE

In the eyes of MG lovers, the MGB was simply ruined by BL's hamfisted makeover, its slinky looks defaced with black rubber and its verve stunted in the name of Californian air quality. The MGB lasted another six years but the company never even bothered to replace it.

# DRESSED UP IN RUBBER, THE MGB JUST DIDN'T DO IT FOR SPORTY TYPES

MG used to use some wonderful advertising slogans in the 1970s. 'Your mother wouldn't like it' and 'You can do it in an MG' left you in no uncertainty as to what a blast through the country lanes in a burbling little MG roadster was to be followed by.

And why not? After all, owning an MG sports car was all about squirting around in a sexy little number and having all your senses assailed by the right sounds, feelings, sights, even smells.

Still, the MGB's fortune was sought in the USA – where it was a big seller – and when in 1975 that country set stringent new safety demands, the classic English two-seater had to smarten up its act.

So British Leyland raised the car's suspension by 1.5in and fitted it with horribly ugly black rubber bumpers so it could pass impact tests. It detuned the engine so it wouldn't

The raised ride height ruined the handling and the big black rubber bumpers messed up the looks, but the MGB soldiered on for another six years.

pollute so much. And the interior received a makeover apparently by the chief designer at MFI, with lurid orange seats replacing the snappy black ones.

The end result was a car with horrible 'tiptoe' roadholding while a wheezy old engine had to haul lots more weight around, which stunted an already – by the standards of the day – leisurely performance. A couple of years later, the suspension was tweaked so the car's road manners were improved.

But the 'rubber bumper' period MGB – and, for that matter, the Midget too – were for years a low point in MG's august history.

The MGB, as they say, had a good innings but the British Leyland malaise of the 1970s saw it decline rapidly. Still, these two are bowled over by their GT.

## ON THE PLUS SIDE

Fie to those purists! Most sports car fiends like nothing more than wind in the air and a growling exhaust note, and these the later model MGB has in spades. It also happens to be a far more comfortable car with a better dashboard and controls, so on no account let that rubber put you off.

Before and after: the MGB (right) was introduced in 1962 and pensioned off in 1981; yet in 1992 the car was re-launched as the MG RV8 (left).

## THE MG MAESTRO 1600

### ON THE MINUS SIDE

As Project LC10, the Maestro had been a long time in the planning, and was supposed to build on the Metro's success. Unfortunately, the MG version – supposedly the range's image leader – had a terrible engine that rendered it a nightmare to even the most patient of owners

# MUSIC, MAESTRO, PLEASE . . . BUT NOT FROM THIS TUNELESS ENGINE

If you can remember anything about the Maestro then it will be its talking dashboard. The synthesised voice of actress Nicolette McKenzie talked to drivers from a computer buried behind the facia, warning them about their fuel consumption and failed lightbulbs. It was a typically tacky BL gimmick that was quickly dropped despite inspiring a host of tabloid stories and featuring in a storyline of Channel Four's new soap *Brookside*.

A more pressing problem for the Maestro, however, was the appalling 1.6-litre R Series engine, fitted to the top Vanden Plas model and, as here, the 'sporty' MG version.

It was rough, it wouldn't re-start when hot, it seemed incapable of delivering its top power of 103bhp, and its twin Weber carburettors were temperamental. This engine was a dog, and BL's own development engineers had been dead against rushing it into production.

The rest of the car was basically sound, with coil spring suspension, decent handling and plenty of room inside.

This is the MG they don't want you to recall, the first MG Maestro with the terrible 1.6-litre power unit the engineers warned against.

Fastest

RATED **9th** OUT OF **10**

Max speed: 111 mph

However, the Maestro was an odd size, bigger than an Escort and smaller than a Sierra. It was also far from handsome, with its filed-off corners and flat grille; the MG insignia, with strange, square-patterned alloy wheels, red seatbelts and tacked-on black plastic spoilers, was hardly pretty either.

BL knew the car was well sub-standard and only a tiny number of MG Maestros were sold before, after a mere nine months on sale, the MG was quietly discontinued. It was then relaunched later in 1984 with a fuel-injected 2-litre engine and a five-speed gearbox borrowed from the Volkswagen Golf . . . and minus Nicolette's annoying drawl.

After just a year on sale, the car was re-engined and re-launched as the MG Maestro 2.0EFi shown here, and a punchy performer it proved too.

### ON THE PLUS SIDE

Once the R Series motor had been jettisoned, this car was immediately transformed. The MG Maestro EFi was powerful and fast and had surprisingly good roadholding. The Golf GTi got a credible and characterful British rival, albeit a little too late in the day to salvage the Maestro's tainted reputation.

Daftest Features

RATED **4th** OUT OF **10**

Ghastly talking dashboard

Computers check Maestro build quality in the Cowley factory; ironically, the car's 'talking' in-dash computer sparked tabloid tittering.

## THE MINI CLUBMAN

AT A GLANCE

**Built**: 1969–82 in Longbridge, Birmingham, West Midlands

**Engine**: four-cylinder, 998/1098cc

**Top speed**: 82mph

**Price when new**: £720

**Number produced**: 473,189

A family of five is a bit of a squeeze in any Mini, and BL's pointless Clubman facelift did nothing to improve the cramped conditions.

# A REAL SQUARE AMONG THE RACY 'MINI' BABY BOOMERS

You wouldn't expect to find the Mini in a book like this, I hope. Britain's best-loved and best-selling small car, a trend-setting design classic, and a vehicle that more than fulfilled its brief, the Mini was so hard to improve upon that it managed to survive pretty much unchanged for an astonishing 42 years.

The Mini Clubman, however, I believe qualifies as one of the worst cars ever sold in Britain because it failed utterly to add to the Mini's qualities. In fact, from the vantage point of the early 21st century, the Clubman seems utterly pointless.

For the Mini, despite its greatness, had several failings. It was noisy, cramped and uncomfortable. None of these things are different in the Clubman. The principal change was an utterly facile, squared-up bonnet, which simply ruined the Mini's extraordinarily recognisable shape. While it looked vaguely like the bigger Austin Maxi, it also messed up the car's aerodynamics.

A slightly more modern dashboard and some very slightly more upmarket trimmings completed the package. Oh, yes,

### ON THE MINUS SIDE

There is absolutely no advantage to the Clubman over other contemporary Minis: the car was simply a cynical exercise by (allegedly) ex-Ford BL managers to update the Mini in the cheapest, tackiest way possible. Still, concentrating on all the wrong things was what they turned out to be best at. . . .

The Mini Clubman estate boasted van-like practicality, nimble handling, and a thick stripe of wood-effect Formica along its sides.

one more thing: the estate version had some Formica-style fake wood strips on the side.

The car even destroyed the Mini's sporty legend, after the Clubman-shaped 1275GT replaced the Cooper.

There's never been much of a cogent explanation as to why British Leyland bothered designing the Clubman; after all, it offered none of the practicality of more modern Mini rivals like the Renault 5 and Fiat 127. However, when the Metro came along in 1980, the Clubman was quickly discontinued . . . leaving the traditional Mini to soldier on for another 22 years with its original, familiar snub nose.

## ON THE PLUS SIDE

The Clubman boxy snout makes getting at the car's engine, the distributor especially, somewhat less of a back-breaker than in a 'normal' Mini; the interior is a touch more civilised too. And the 1275GT is a pocket-sized fun car with plenty of 1970s retro-chic, if you can find one that hasn't rusted away.

Best Selling

RATED **8th** OUT OF **10**

Sold: 473,189

The Mini refused to roll over and die: the Clubman was discontinued in 1981 but the snub-nosed original lived on for another two decades.

**Built**: 1965–95 in Westbury, Wiltshire and Oldham, Lancashire
**Engine**: four-cylinder 848/1098/1275cc
**Top speed**: 100mph
**Price when new**: £199 as basic kit
**Number produced**: 1,264

## ON THE MINUS SIDE

Sports cars should, as part of their DNA, be pretty, but the Mini-Marcos is without doubt one of the ugliest ever. The low-rent image was not helped by the fact that most were sold as kit cars, with the final finish reflecting the constructor's own aesthetic standards. . . .

# MAKES ALL THE RIGHT MOVES BUT LOOKS LIKE A DOG'S BREAKFAST

The Mini-Marcos did a sterling job at Le Mans in 1967. Okay, it didn't win, but it was the only British car to complete the gruelling 24-hour race. The two French drivers were, understandably, elated, and spent the evening afterwards in champagne-soaked celebration. The following day, however, they were in for a shock: the plucky little car had been stolen overnight, and it was never seen or heard of again.

I mention this event because I feel these two chaps deserve some credit for spending 24 hours wedged inside one of the most claustrophobic and cramped sports cars of all time.

The car was a sound idea, a baby Marcos using the Mini's subframes in a glassfibre monocoque. It was simple, light and had excellent handling and performance, thanks to the Mini's front-wheel drive and transverse engine location.

However, while the body style might have looked all right on the back of an envelope, and was quite a wind-cheater, in the flesh it looked crude and ugly – something that had been made from old suitcases and odds and ends from the garden shed. The early cars had sliding windows, but even the later models never looked as though their panels fitted properly. Their owners, presumably, were more preoccupied with sensations than aesthetic considerations.

Over 1,000 of the cars were sold, most of them as kits and with any variant of the Mini's A Series engine, in the Mini-Marcos's long life and varied ownership. Even the attempt to replace it with the professional-looking Midas in 1978 didn't stop the car being revived in 1991 – incredibly, after pressure from Japan for more.

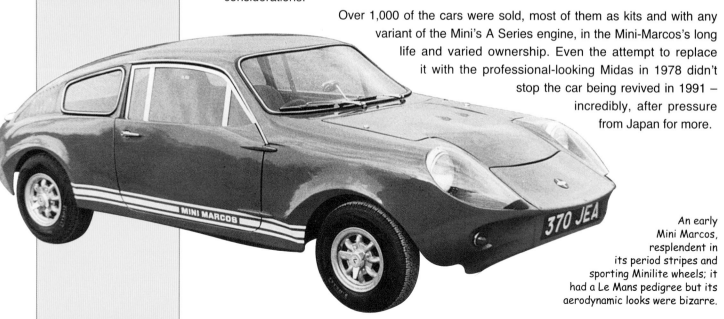

An early Mini Marcos, resplendent in its period stripes and sporting Minilite wheels; it had a Le Mans pedigree but its aerodynamic looks were bizarre.

In 1975 Mini Marcos production moved to Oldham and it gained a prominent 'mouth' on its bonnet to aid engine cooling; inexplicably, the car continued to sell.

## ON THE PLUS SIDE

The Mini-Marcos is one of the forgotten fun cars of the 1960s, with all the emphasis on the driving experience. So sign here if it's low-priced exhilaration you want, coupled with extremely low spares costs and fuel economy. And, of course, a noble Le Mans heritage.

In 1991, demand from Japan resulted in a Mini Marcos relaunch, with 64 examples leaving Westbury for their barmy Far Eastern owners.

**Built**: 1963–67 in Malvern, Worcestershire
**Engine**: four-cylinder, 2138cc
**Top speed**: 110mph
**Price when new**: £1,275
**Number produced**: 26

# MORGAN LOST THE PLOT WITH THIS WEIRD PLASTIC COUPE

Picture a Morgan and the image that springs to most minds is as traditionally English as Yorkshire pudding or red pillar boxes. Wind in the hair, grit in the teeth, and vintage simplicity in all things – from the separate, hand-beaten wings to the outside spare wheel and trio of tiny windscreen wipers. Flying goggles are a must.

You don't imagine a stylish two-seater coupe with – gulp – plastic bodywork.

But that's just what Morgan dished up to a disbelieving public in 1964 under the name of Plus Four Plus (crumbs, even the quintessentially British trouser reference was given the '60s treatment).

Boss Peter Morgan was afraid his loyal customers, who'd been buying basically the same car since the first four-wheeled Morgan was launched in 1936, would one day desert him for more modish pastures. Hence the pretty new face – albeit on the identical Morgan chassis with its Triumph TR4 engine.

Obviously, using that antediluvian item, incorporating Morgan's trademark sliding pillar front suspension, with a closed bodyshell did not result in a refined car. And the styling, with its odd, pinched little 'bubble' roof from beneath which the two passengers peered, wasn't especially elegant.

Peter Morgan's calculations were incorrect: in fact, there was an immediate upsurge in orders for the classic item that's continued unabated ever since. Just 26 Plus Four Pluses were sold in three years.

The first four-wheeled Morgan sports car was introduced in 1936 and the cars have barely changed since, to the delight of the company's ultra-loyal customers.

**Fastest**
RATED **10th** OUT OF **10**
Max speed:
110 mph

Curious, bubble-shaped roof gave the Plus Four Plus a claustrophobic feeling for driver and passenger; bodywork was made from glassfibre.

**Worst Selling**
RATED **6th** OUT OF **10**
Number Sold: 26

Now Morgan is tampering with its fundamentals once more, after announcing its radical, BMW-powered Aero 8. The orders have poured in but it remains to be seen whether its customers, so in love with the company's ancient traditions, will really warm to another 'new' Morgan.

## ON THE PLUS SIDE

You can't blame Morgan for having a go at something a bit more modern in the decade of free love and moon walks. The car could be just the thing for those who like a vintage drive but are also loathe to give up the creature comforts of more modern sportsters.

## ON THE MINUS SIDE

The latest Aero 8 retains the fundamental charm of its illustrious Morgan forebears but the Plus Four Plus chucked it all away with its pseudo-Lotus styling. Thankfully, a stuffy cabin and swoopy plastic panels have never been seen again on a car from the hallowed Malvern Link factory.

Restrained artwork from Morgan's Plus Four Plus brochure did nothing to help sales – 'sports enthusiasts' actually stuck to their traditional models.

THE *NEW* CAR
FOR THE SPORTS ENTHUSIAST

𝕸𝖔𝖗𝖌𝖆𝖓
'PLUS FOUR PLUS'

The Morgan Aero 8, with its high-tech chassis and BMW V8 engine, is Morgan's most radical car since the Plus Four Plus – it's destined to be rather more popular.

# AN ITALIAN JOB THE ITALIANS WOULD MUCH RATHER FORGET

The Morris Ital 1.7SLX estate at least had welcome carrying capacity but by the time this example was made in 1983 the car was woefully old-fashioned.

I f you politely request it, the Italian design house Ital Design will give you a booklet that shows every one of its production cars. If you didn't know it already, you will find the company, founded and led by Giorgetto Giugiaro, was responsible for the looks of the Volkswagen Golf, the Fiat Uno, the Lotus Esprit and the Lexus GS300.

Only one car has ever borne the design bureau's name. That car is the Morris Ital. Tellingly, though, it is nowhere to be seen in Ital Design's promotional literature. This sad machine has been airbrushed out of Ital's history. The marque itself vanished 17 years ago. And surviving Morris Itals are few and far between.

The car began life as the 1971 Morris Marina, a model afflicted with terrible understeer, feeble performance and Morris Minor-derived lever-arm front suspension. Saloon, coupé, estate, van, pick-up, A, B or O Series engines, multiple trim levels; every Marina was a mediocre car, equipped as they were with just four-speed gearboxes.

By 1982, the Marina was very stodgy fare indeed. Hence the Ital Design tart-up to give it two more years of life. On went a slanting nose, new bumpers and restyled tail lights, and the interior was tinkered with to make it mildly less depressing. The coupé was dropped, and the TV commercials implied the Ital was thrusting and dynamic. Which it most certainly was not.

When the car finally came to the end of its ridiculously long life, Austin Rover took the opportunity to bin the Morris name as well. It was a sad end to a great British badge, but probably for the best.

## ON THE MINUS SIDE

Like an ageing, daytime soap star, the Ital was past its best and had had one facelift too many. It was actually remarkable that it had survived so long because the Marina on which it was based was considered a poor car even when it was brand new 11 years previously.

Hmm, not one that Giorgetto Giugiaro wants to be associated with – the Morris Ital has been carefully airbrushed off his company's CV. . . .

A BL employee fits the sparkplugs to an Ital in the Cowley factory; this was to be the last car to bear the Morris name – and Cowley now makes the new Mini.

Morris Marina coupés enjoy a bit of spirited fun on launch day in 1971; when the model turned into the Ital nine years later the coupé was dropped.

## ON THE PLUS SIDE

The Ital, and indeed the Marina, are simple motors. There's nothing in the way of fancy gadgets or computer-controlled electronic wizardry to stop them in their tracks, and the estate in particular was always practical and good value. It's just the dreaded rust that's seen off so many of them.

**Built:** 1969–75 in Moscow, Russia
**Engine:** four-cylinder, 1478cc
**Top speed:** 90mph
**Price when new:** £717
**Number produced:** unknown

### ON THE MINUS SIDE

The Moskvich was not good for you in a crash: once that had been proven by consumers' groups there was no hope for this third-rate Russian saloon. Still, if the press hadn't done for it then regulations on exhaust emissions and other environmental matters would certainly have seen the Moskvich off soon afterwards.

# IT'S JUST NOT SAFE TO GO OUT (IN A MOSKVICH, THAT IS)

The Moskvich 412 could reach 90mph all too quickly. Amazingly, that made this bargain-basement Russian saloon a racing car in the hands of one Tony Lanfranchi. During the early 1970s, he entered one into standard saloon car races where the car qualified within the lowest price category because its heavily subsidised price meant it cost less than a Mini. With racing numbers on its doors, the car could be seen skimming its doorhandles on the corners of minor UK race tracks.

The Moskvich 412 was a conventional four-door saloon (the estate was called the 427) with an overhead-camshaft 1500cc engine. This unit is a straight rip-off of BMW's 1.5-litre unit, and Moskvich fans (yes, they do exist) say some parts are actually interchangeable.

The car was a big hit in Britain when it was launched here in 1969 because it was so ridiculously cheap. In the metal-for-your-money stakes there was nothing to touch it – a Cortina-sized family car for the price of a cramped Mini – and sales soared. It was a bit coarse, but so what?

However, its role as a buyer's favourite was short. In 1973, the Consumers Association issued a damning report that declared the Moskvich dangerously unsafe. The particular car it drove had badly adjusted brakes and steering, but its main thrust was that the spearing effects of various parts of the dashboard would be lethal for passengers in an impact.

BBC1's current affairs programme *Nationwide* ran a big story on the report, and Moskvich sales evaporated overnight, forcing the marque out of Britain altogether in 1976.

With an engine copied from BMW and typical Russian toughness, the Moskvich found many buyers, until safety fears killed British sales stone dead.

The Moskvich estate was called the 427, and this 1973 example cost just £799.06 all-in – this was just a few pounds more than a Mini, dangerous dashboard protuberances notwithstanding.

A novel Moskvich detail designed to thwart thieves was a petrol cap hidden behind a rear number plate held in place by the bootlid when closed.

I'll wager there are no Moskvich vans still in service in the UK, and precious few even as spruce as this rotting remnant.

## ON THE PLUS SIDE

Any motor car that's built to survive winters in the Soviet Union must have something about it. The Moskvich is a no-nonsense piece of kit, and some fans say that the hysteria over the car's potential safety hazards was over-done. It's no sports car but, then, it never set out to be one.

**Built:** 1986–91 in Yokohama, Japan
**Engine:** four-cylinder, 1597/1598/1809cc
**Top speed:** 128mph
**Price when new:** £11,195 (1.6GSX)
**Number produced:** unknown

Fastest

RATED **4th** OUT OF **10**

Max speed:
128 mph

Just take a look at this Nissan: not what most people would describe as sporting, is it? And not helped by a tacky bodykit apparently attached outside Halfords.

# SPORTING PRETENSIONS BUT IT'S DEFINITELY NOT EYE CANDY

Two things: first, there are a lot of extremely mediocre 1970s, '80s and '90s Nissans at which to have a pop – Cherrys, Sunnys, Violets, Bluebirds, Laurels . . . the daft names are no doubt familiar. Second, there is actually nothing fundamentally terrible about the 1986–91 Sunny Coupé.

So why on earth single out this motoring innocent for a bashing?

Well, I ask you – just take a look at the thing. Isn't this just the ugliest 'sporting' car you've ever seen?

The car was part of the second-generation front-wheel drive Sunny line-up, which also numbered hatchbacks, saloons and estates, and like them the Coupé was an uninspired exercise in straight-lined design, with not a curve, an interesting aspect nor an even mildly emotive feature to tantalise the potential driver.

Apart from the basic model, there was the ZX with twin-cam 122bhp and later 16-valve 128bhp GTI engines. That meant some of these cars could reach 128mph.

That was fast, and the handling was just about okay too, but the ride was awful and the tacky body kit Nissan glued on to the ZX did it no favours at all – the spoilers and side skirts look no better than cheapies you might pick up at Halfords on a rainy Sunday morning and glue on to the car yourself.

Amazingly, you could have had either the excellent Golf GTi or 205 GTi for the same money as the ZX Twin-Cam.

But just before you turn the page in disgust at seeing a perfectly acceptable car condemned, give this Nissan one long, last look. Is it not absolutely dreadful?

Ugliest

RATED **5th** OUT OF **10**

The dreariest-looking sporting car ever?

## ON THE MINUS SIDE

Not sure if I've rammed the point home yet: the Nissan Sunny Coupé is a truly ugly, unattractive car, and not one that's at all worthy to carry a sporting tag. It's one of the many confused-image cars that have led to Nissan being bailed out by style-conscious Renault.

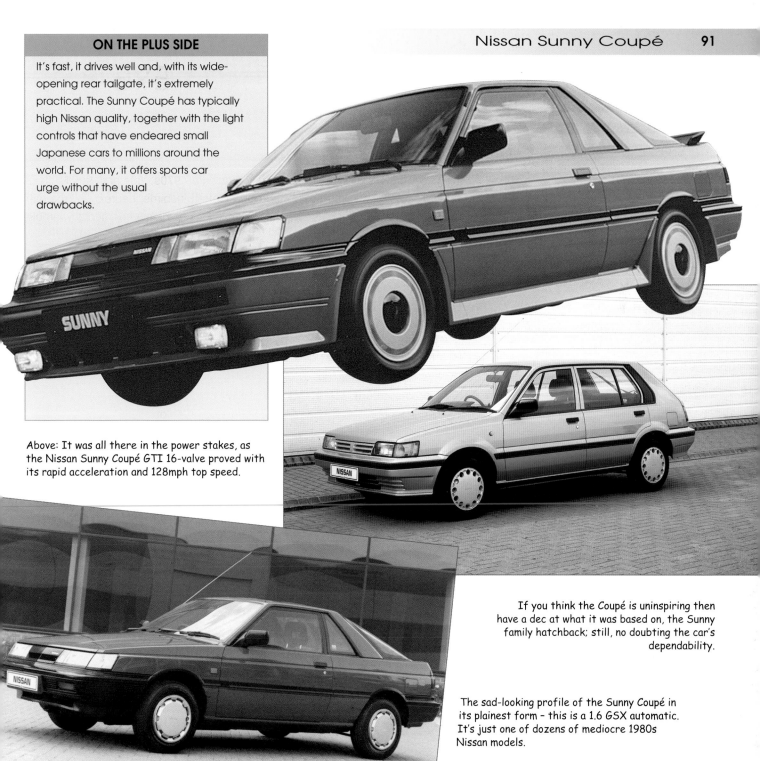

## ON THE PLUS SIDE

It's fast, it drives well and, with its wide-opening rear tailgate, it's extremely practical. The Sunny Coupé has typically high Nissan quality, together with the light controls that have endeared small Japanese cars to millions around the world. For many, it offers sports car urge without the usual drawbacks.

Above: It was all there in the power stakes, as the Nissan Sunny Coupé GTI 16-valve proved with its rapid acceleration and 128mph top speed.

If you think the Coupé is uninspiring then have a dec at what it was based on, the Sunny family hatchback; still, no doubting the car's dependability.

The sad-looking profile of the Sunny Coupé in its plainest form – this is a 1.6 GSX automatic. It's just one of dozens of mediocre 1980s Nissan models.

## THE NUFFIELD OXFORD

### AT A GLANCE

**Built**: 1947–55 in Birmingham, West Midlands

**Engine**: four-cylinder, 1802cc

**Top speed**: unknown

**Price when new**: unknown

**Number produced**: 1,800 approx

### ON THE MINUS SIDE

This was a vehicle that was 20 years out of date before it even carried a fare-paying passenger. Presumably, it appealed to grizzled, elderly taxi-men who didn't hold with anything new-fangled, but it can't have been much fun to travel in for either the driver or the passengers.

# LIVING ANTIQUE WASN'T A FARE DEAL ON THE COMFORT FRONT

London's world-famous taxi trade came to be dominated by just one make, Austin, by the late 1940s, despite the fact that Renault had had a stranglehold on the market in the early years of the 20th century, and the Scottish Beardmore had been a popular choice among cabbies in the 1920s and '30s.

Still, the Nuffield Organisation thought it could crack it in 1947 with its Oxford taxicab. It was not, however, strictly a car, being based on a modified Morris Commercial van chassis and fitted with a four-cylinder 1802cc sidevalve engine whose roots went right back to Morris's earliest manufacturing days.

With its underslung axle at the back, rod-operated brakes and old-fashioned 'artillery' wheels, the Oxford provided plenty for taxi drivers

Daftest Features

RATED **5th** OUT OF **10**

One side open to the elements so driver has a constant cold

A chilly day's work was guaranteed for the driver of the Nuffield Oxford taxicab – there was no door on the nearside to make loading luggage easier.

to moan about (as if they needed the excuse) – this was definitely a second-class-citizen machine that couldn't be further from the cutting edge of technology. There wasn't even a window on the driver's side in early models!

However, it was robust: the first prototype, built in 1940, covered over 100,000 miles throughout the war years. It then hit London's streets for field trials in 1947 and, with experienced Beardmore soon marketing the Oxford instead of developing its own new model, it became fairly commonplace.

However, when Austin took over Nuffield to form the British Motor Corporation in 1952, the two taxis found themselves jostling at the corporate rank and, unsurprisingly, the Oxford lost the fight. The last of around 1,800 was made in 1955. A handful was also sold to straight-laced, Victorian types as Wolseley Oxford six-light limousines. Survivors today are very rare indeed.

A 1926 Morris Oxford tourer: the Oxford cab was similar in many ways to such vintage machinery, sharing, for instance, old-fashioned 'artillery'-style wheels.

## ON THE PLUS SIDE

The London taxi trade is a law unto itself, having its origins in the days of horse-drawn vehicles. It's steeped in its own traditions and arcane laws, and new taxis don't come along often. The few Oxfords that went into service probably did the job, and kept thousands of American tourists happy.

We forget today that the Nuffield Organisation was among Britain's biggest car producers in the 1930s; here the one-millionth car is donated to Guys Hospital by William Morris (on left) in 1937.

**Built**: 1973 in Edmonton, north London
**Engine**: six-cylinder, 4235cc
**Top speed**: unknown
**Price when new**: £8,500
**Number produced**: 2

### ON THE MINUS SIDE

A Jaguar XJ6 is rather a good car, but dismember it and graft on an aluminium body of dubious style and engineering integrity, and this is the sort of thing you get. Gerald Ronson had a lucky escape when the gathering fuel crisis thwarted his hopes to be an independent car maker.

# AFTER THE GUINNESS AFFAIR, HERE'S RONSON'S OTHER SCANDAL

Gerald Ronson has certainly tasted the spice of life – from running property-to-petrol-stations group Heron, one of Britain's biggest privately owned companies, to doing bird in Ford Open Prison for his part in the Guinness share-support scandal. Nowadays he's planning a skyscraper for London. He's been a car manufacturer too. Well, almost.

But for the 1974 oil crisis, his Sedanca might now be as common a sight in monied London as the Mercedes-Benz SL. It was inspired by Ronson's own personal car of the time, a Lamborghini Espada, and was intended to provide four sumptuous seats in a swish, British-made coupé.

The very un-Italian part was the complete Jaguar XJ6 floorpan and purring engine underneath. Inside, it was a cocoon of coffee-coloured Dralon and tan suede leather. Hidden in the driver's door was a silver-backed hairbrush.

The car was penned by a youthful, self-taught independent car designer called Chris Humberstone, and was fashioned by a tiny north London coachbuilder, Williams & Pritchard, which derived most of its business from making racing car bodies. Starting at the Jaguar's scuttle, the company lovingly attached the all-aluminium body by hand. It was not a particularly pretty sight.

With a price tag of £8,500, the Sedanca looked somewhat of a costly gas-guzzler and all 80 orders that Ronson's smart HR Owen showrooms had taken were quickly cancelled.

It was the Lamborghini Espada that inspired the Owen Sedanca, and Gerald Ronson's money that backed the project – prematurely curtailed after the 1970s fuel crisis.

Two cars were eventually made for Arab brothers to use on their Oxfordshire country estate, costing tens of thousands of pounds, yet one was sold at auction in October 1994 for just £3,740, less than the price of a then-current Lada.

The Sedanca takes shape in the north London workshops of Williams & Pritchard; the entire body was hand-beaten in aluminium using traditional coachbuilding methods.

**ON THE PLUS SIDE**

You have to admire the enterprise and ingenuity of Chris Humberstone and his patron. The wedge-shaped Sedanca was extremely trendy at the time and, with a bit more development and a weather eye on quality, could have given Italian and German supercars a run for their money.

Worst Selling

RATED 1st OUT OF 10

Number Sold: 2

An outsider would never have known it but the Owen Sedanca was built on the floorpan of the Jaguar XJ6, with much of the strength coming from the Jag's scuttle structure.

**Built**: 1975–85 in Byfleet, Surrey

**Engine**: six-cylinder, 4235cc, V12, 5343cc

**Top speed**: 135mph

**Price when new**: £39,049

**Number produced**: 60

Fastest

RATED **1st** OUT OF **10**

Max speed: 135 mph

### ON THE MINUS SIDE

To vintage car enthusiasts, an appalling travesty of motoring heritage, with vulgar styling, inconsistent detailing, and a rip-off price tag. Far more likely to appear in an upmarket porn flick than at the Bugatti Owners' Club annual rally; thankfully, most of them are too far away from the UK to incite rioting.

Look carefully and you'll be able to recognise the doors from an Austin 1800 making up a big part of the Panther Deville's carefully constructed body.

# VULGAR BUGATTI PASTICHE FOR THE RIYADH SCHOOL RUN

The 'replicar' was a peculiar trend that started in the USA in 1964 when Excalibur and Ruger revealed their beautifully made copies of the Mercedes-Benz SSK and Blower Bentley respectively, only both powered by modern, untemperamental engines. Perhaps as a reaction to the 'sameness' of then-current car design, they caught on – particularly for rich violets who weren't too keen on shrinking. Tommy Steele was Britain's best known Excalibur driver.

Britain joined in in 1972 with the Panther J72. This was a not-bad Jaguar-powered copy of the beautiful 1930s SS100 sports car. The Panther Deville followed it in 1974, but this time it was more pastiche than tribute.

Sitting on a giant 142in wheelbase, the tubular-framed monster used Jaguar six- and 12-cylinder engines and was supposed to ape the incredible 1930 Bugatti Royale. Real vintage car enthusiasts sneered – especially at the door structure of the Deville saloon, which was pinched wholesale from a humble Austin 1800 and none-too-artfully melded into the overall design.

They were heavy, incredibly expensive, individually customised and of excellent build quality – many of Panther's panelbeaters, coachtrimmers and leatherworkers had lifetime experience in their various crafts. And they were okay to drive, although more suitable for ostentatious cruising than twisty country lanes.

Worst Selling

RATED **9th** OUT OF **10**

Number Sold: 60

About 60 of these handbuilt pimp-mobiles were made until 1985, including a two-door convertible spin-off. The very last example, however, a pink and gold six-door limousine, spoke volumes about the sort of people who commissioned Devilles: the majority went to the Middle East to take part in one-upmanship contests of bad taste with neighbours on the other side of the desert.

With its six doors, side-mounted spare wheels, giant-sized gold bonnet mascot, and pink-and-gold paintwork, this is the ultimate Deville, if you can call it that.

The Deville immortalised on screen: this is a scene from *The Golden Lady*, starring someone called Christina World. Anyone got it on video?

Daftest Features

RATED **6th** OUT OF **10**

Luggage stored in a fake trunk lashed to the back

### ON THE PLUS SIDE

Panther founder Robert Jankel, an ex-fashion designer who entered the car business for kicks, was a fount of offbeat ideas, and the Deville isn't the most outrageous by any means. The car industry is a duller place without his kind, and many of the skills used in building the Deville have virtually died out.

## THE POLSKI-FIAT/ FSO POLONEZ

**Built**: 1977–92 in Warsaw, Poland
**Engine**: four-cylinder, 1265/1481/1598cc
**Top speed**: 96mph
**Price when new**: £3,194
**Number produced**: 440,500

# POLES APART FROM THE BEST OF EUROPE'S FAMILY HATCHBACKS

**W**hen the Polonez made its appearance 23 years ago, it seemed to be the answer to many motorists' prayers: a powerful and handy five-door family hatchback at a very affordable price. Buyers hot-footed it down to Polski-Fiat showrooms to give it a try.

Unfortunately, they were in for a disappointment: pulling up the 'fifth door' revealed a rather major oversight. The Polonez's designers had forgotten to include a folding rear seat, so there was room only for a few carrier bags of shopping. The omission was corrected a few years later, but it was indicative of the shoddy nature of the car and the company.

Fiat helped the Polish Fabryka Samochdow Osobowych (FSO) factory make a modern car by granting it a licence in 1965 to build the Fiat 125 – until then, it had nailed together a version of Russia's Pobeida. The Polski-Fiat 125p did the job but, by 1977, was well past its prime. Hence the Polonez, built to another Fiat design, albeit one never produced in Italy.

Fiat designed the Polonez but never made it themselves. Just one look at its hideous lines tells you why, but it didn't stop the Poles from churning them out.

**Ugliest**
RATED **6th** OUT OF **10**

All the style and class of Warsaw Airport

## ON THE MINUS SIDE

Any value in the low, low British asking price for a Polonez was instantly wiped out by the car's crippling depreciation. Just about any western European car was a better bet even with 50,000 miles on its clock and a few dents. When was the last time you actually saw one?

The suspension juts into the luggage space but at least the rear seats fold down in later Polonez cars – FSO originally 'forgot' to include this critical feature.

The 125p's innards were carried over wholesale, including four-wheel disc brakes, and the artificially low export prices compensated for the car's myriad shortcomings and horrible sensory experiences.

Even Fiat was worried about the product stagnation at FSO – it forced it to stop using the Polski-Fiat name in 1981, after which the cars were renamed FSOs. With no spare capital to invest, the Polonez continued unchanged until 1992, when engines and looks were refreshed and it was renamed the Caro. Production limped on towards the end of the decade, but faded away after Daewoo bought the factory. FSO depreciation in this country meant the car was more likely to be scrapped than sold secondhand.

**Best Selling**

RATED **9th** OUT OF **10**

Sold: 440,500

This is a Polski Fiat 125p, although you could be forgiven for thinking it's a Fiat 125 – the cars are identical, but you can spot the Polish one because of its laughable quality.

## ON THE PLUS SIDE

Anyone who's ever taken delivery of a brand new car will recall the feeling of pride and satisfaction, and the Polonez offered that emotion to Britain's most poverty-stricken motorists. With a big engine, a (latterly) spacious body and low day-to-day running costs, it wasn't all bad.

**Daftest Features**

RATED **7th** OUT OF **10**

Hatchback yes but folding seats - er . . .

This sophisticated-looking product is an FSO Caro pick-up; a few were sold in the UK as cut-price load-luggers, and provided workmanlike service.

**Built**: 1975–81 (Princess), 1982–84 (Ambassador) in Longbridge, Birmingham

**Engine**: four-cylinder, 1798/1695/1993; six-cylinder, 2227cc

**Top speed**: 110mph (Princess), 100mph (Ambassador)

**Price when new**: £2,237

**Number produced**: 205,842 (Princess), 43,500 (Ambassador)

# PRINCESS HAD A SHORT REIGN DESPITE TECHNICAL GENIUS

In the popular argot of the old car world, the 1964–74 Austin, Morris and Wolseley 1800/2200 models are known as 'Landcrabs' because of their ungainly width, wheels at each corner and massive, central, passenger compartment. Designed by the great Sir Alec Issigonis along similar Mini principles, they were the first large family cars with front-wheel drive. Roomy and sophisticated, they struggled against equivalent Vauxhalls and Fords – buyers found them strangely off-putting.

British Leyland's solution was to ditch the styling and go super-trendy, with the first wedge-shaped saloon that your dad could actually buy. The sharp-lined, high-tailed shape was from the pen of Harris Mann, who also created the look of the Allegro and TR7, and the new range made its debut in 1975.

There was one drawback: although the car looked as if it was a modern hatchback, it in fact had a conventional boot. Early anecdotal evidence suggested quality was suspect, while the Hydragas suspension, kind to passengers over potholes, was apt to make you feel car-sick on long journeys.

BL took the unusual step of ditching its three makes after just nine months, creating the Princess marque to supplant them. The Princess 2

'Refinement to suit the successful executive and family man', said BL of the Princess 2200HL you see here. Unfortunately, he tended to prefer the more conventional Ford offerings.

### ON THE MINUS SIDE

It might have looked up-to-the-minute but the Princess was a far less versatile car than the similar Renault 16 – which was a full 10 years older. Gas-filled suspension was a dubious plus, and the Ambassador was a case of too little, too late. Plus, they all have 1970s BL build quality.

It must have looked pretty darned modern in 1976 but the interior of the Princess, here a 1700L, today seems to be a frightening cavern of shiny black plastic.

Originally, the Princess-shape cars were sold as Austins, Morrises or, shown here, a Wolseley. They were replaced by the Princess marque after nine months, when Wolseley died forever.

in 1978 brought new four-cylinder engines. However, they didn't take the opportunity to introduce a fifth door until 1982, when – in typically confusing form – Princess was killed off and the car became an Austin again, this time on Ambassador.

Despite a new, more aerodynamic nose, an extra side window and other useful changes, the basic car had already had three failed bites at the success cherry and, by the time the Ambassador was discontinued in 1984, it was a motoring relic.

The Princess was stretched into an inelegant limousine by Halifax firm Woodall Nicholson, and named the Kirklees.

## ON THE PLUS SIDE

One way or another, British Leyland managed to squeeze 20 years out of its Landcrab 'platform', and for anyone seeking a car with enormous space for occupants, excellent roadholding, and a posher image from the Americanised tinniness of contemporary Fords and Vauxhalls, they were all worth a look.

**Built**: 1981–82 in Woking, Surrey
**Engine**: four-cylinder, 1602/1750cc
**Top speed**: 106mph
**Price when new**: £12,995
**Number produced**: 40 approx

# GADGETS DIDN'T MAKE THE RITZ A CRACKER

Chris Humberstone, the peripatetic designer behind the Owen Sedanca, popped up regularly attached to other projects before his premature death in 1996. Although many of these extravagant creations were individually built for novelty-crazed Arab princes, none was quite so strange as the Rapport Ritz.

Rapport was an upmarket car showroom on London's Park Lane, where rich Middle Eastern customers were wont to drop in while staying at the nearby Grosvenor House or Dorchester hotels and splash some cash. But the Ritz was aimed at Londoners.

The car was based on the Honda Accord and intended as a smart and economical mini-limousine for the man- or woman-about-town. The bits you might have expected were all there, like automatic transmission, power steering, full air-con and an interior liberally plastered with wood and Connolly leather.

However, outside, Humberstone fitted his own boot treatment and front wings, made from glassfibre, together with a deep front spoiler and a curious front aerofoil that made the car sleek by day but could be raised electrically at night so the four headlights could do their stuff. It was a pointless gadget on a rather pointless motor car.

The snatched snapshot might be a bit fuzzy but it's easy to recognise the Honda Accord basis of this Rapport Ritz, one of around 40 examples sold.

## ON THE MINUS SIDE

In the car world, it's very tricky to turn one thing into another, and there was no hiding the Ritz's roots. The glassfibre panels and fancy interior added little to the Accord's already excellent qualities, and the electric aerofoil was something that was bound to go wrong sooner or later.

Daftest Features

RATED **8th** OUT OF **10**

Electric aerofoil raises when headlights are on, ruining aerodynamics

The unique selling point of the Ritz was its re-styled nose, complete with strange front aerofoil, that could be raised electrically when the headlights were switched on.

KDC 716W

Some 40 of these strange little cars were built, all four-doors although a three-door version and a convertible were illustrated in catalogues. Some were turbocharged.

The idea had been tried before by Panther, which used a Triumph Dolomite as a basis for its Rio but, as then, customers fought shy of spending such a large amount (over twice the price of a standard Accord) on what was basically a heavily modified Japanese family car. Rapport's rapid descent into bankruptcy in 1982 put an end to the project anyway.

Here's a picture of the standard, unadorned Accord saloon, the starting point for the Ritz. The Chris Humberstone-penned transformation more than doubled the Accord's price.

## ON THE PLUS SIDE

You have to remember that few small cars offered a complete luxury package in 1981 like the Ritz's – today it would seem pointless to spend so much just to be 'different' but back then the car had something special, and the electric aerofoil was an amusing toy to show off to your friends.

Worst Selling

RATED **8th** OUT OF **10**

Number Sold: 40

Panther had tried a similar exercise in 1975, when it used the Triumph Dolomite as the base car for its Rio.

**Built:** 1973–82 in Tamworth, Staffordshire
**Engine:** four-cylinder, 748/848cc
**Top speed:** 80mph
**Price when new:** £801
**Number produced:** 88,000

## ON THE MINUS SIDE

Reliant knew for years that its typical customer was a stubborn ex-miner who'd never bothered to update his motorbike licence. Obviously, this was a dwindling breed – most people wouldn't be seen dead in a wobbly, uncomfortable Robin or any other three-wheeler – and the car lived on long after its time had gone.

# THE WIDEBOY, THE EX-MINER AND A NUTTY BRITISH INSTITUTION

A fiscal loophole in British law allowed the Reliant three-wheeler to flourish for over 60 years. A little-visited page of the lawbook states that a 'tricycle' is classed as a motorbike so long as it keeps its unladen weight down to 500kg. That means the owner pays half a car's road tax, can drive it on a motorbike licence and, with such featherlightness, revel in tiny fuel consumption.

Tom Williams worked for the Raleigh bike company in Nottingham, and in 1935 bought the manufacturing rights to its three-wheeled Safety Seven car. He set up shop in his Tamworth

The original Reliant Robin made its debut in 1973, and was a major improvement on the Regal model it replaced, being styled by a professional design company, Ogle.

The Robin name had such a following that it reappeared in 1990 on this new three-wheeler design; the company's customers were loyal but slowly dwindled away.

ROBIN LX

Everyone thinks TV's Del Boy Trotter drives a Robin van but actually it's a Regal, like this one.

garden shed, and within months was making three-wheeled 'Reliant' vans, powered by Austin Seven engines.

By 1952 he'd introduced a four-seater passenger car version; four years later it gained glassfibre bodywork. In 1962, the new Reliant Regal boasted Reliant's own, light alloy 600cc engine.

Other three-wheelers fell by the wayside, but Reliant went from strength to strength. In 1974 a firm of proper product designers, Ogle, redesigned its staple three-wheeled car. The resulting 70mpg Robin proved even more successful than its predecessors, especially during 1970s fuel crises. Even Princess Anne had one.

But Reliant's image was badly tarnished when worries about the cars' safety and stability surfaced in the press, and the Robin was replaced by the Rialto in 1982. However, the Robin name was revived between 1990 and 2000, and production has just resumed in Suffolk.

By the way, David Jason's portrayal of Peckham wideboy Del Trotter in TV's *Only Fools & Horses* is assisted by a Regal van, and not a Robin as people often think.

Most Handy

RATED **8th** OUT OF **10**

Perfect for nipping around town with the minimum of outlay

# NEW BRITISH SPORTS CAR BLADE WAS ANYTHING BUT SHARP

## THE RELIANT SCIMITAR SS1

### AT A GLANCE

**Built**: 1984–89 in Tamworth, Staffordshire

**Engine**: four-cylinder, 1296/1392/1596/1809cc

**Top speed**: 126mph (1800Ti)

**Price when new**: £7,240

**Number produced**: 1,507

Filling this book with the various products of the Reliant Motor Company is a real temptation, but few British cars have ever been as compromised as the Reliant Scimitar SS1, a car that enthusiasts awaited with keen interest before its 1984 unveiling.

With two-seater MGs and Triumphs now fading into history, Reliant had promised us a return to British sports car roots – a simple two-seater for country lane frolics and wind-in-the-hair refreshment.

The Scimitar SS1, however, was truly a disappointment.

Reassuringly traditional in its front-engine, rear drive layout, with an excellent tubular chassis, and employing parts from Ford and other low-maintenance, household names, it should have been a winner. There was even some heritage – Reliant had been building sports cars, from the Sabre to the Scimitar GTE, for yonks.

The dismay was in the styling. It was the work of one-time Italian maestro Giovanni Michelotti (he had penned the Triumph Spitfire and TR4), but it was also his last effort; he was dying of skin cancer as he completed it, and Reliant apparently got the design for almost nothing.

No doubt it looked funky as a design sketch. But after Reliant's engineers turned it into reality, it was horrible: lines in all the wrong places, glaring

Weird looks, thanks to usually reliable Italian designer Michelotti, blighted the Reliant Scimitar SS1 from day one – check out those odd lines and uneven panel gaps.

### ON THE MINUS SIDE

If ever there was a golden opportunity to revive the small sports car, then Reliant had it in the mid-1980s. The fact that the ship was spoilt for a hap'orth of tar showed just what an amateurish outfit the company was. And then, of course, along came the Mazda MX-5. . . .

Ugliest

RATED **7th** OUT OF **10**

Droopy roadster with appalling panel fit

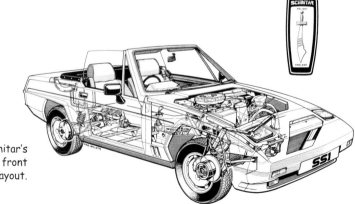

Cutaway drawing shows the Scimitar's clever construction and traditional front engine/rear drive layout.

panel gaps, ugly pop-up headlamps, and nothing to make the heart beat faster with desire – a sports car prerequisite.

There was a low-insurance 1.3-litre version for starters, but Michelotti's droopy bonnet didn't allow room for the Ford XR3i engine – so in went a 1.6-litre Ford with carburettors. The later 1800Ti with Nissan turbo power at least allowed keen drivers to exploit the car's satisfying handling and road manners but, by then, the SS1's chance had passed.

## ON THE PLUS SIDE

Okay, so the car's no looker, but all the other ingredients are there – and the turbocharged 1800Ti is a little cracker. Anyway, a 1990 makeover that turned the car into the Scimitar Sabre added a touch of design neatness. They're all rare, collectible and interesting cars in a time of increasing automotive anonymity.

The car wasn't much happier from behind; this is the 1800Ti, with turbocharged Nissan power, which offered sparkling performance to distract you from its dodgy aesthetics.

Fastest

RATED **5th** OUT OF **10**

Max speed: 126 mph

The Scimitar's lines were cleaned up in 1990 by freelance designer William Towns to create the Scimitar Sabre; alas, the Mazda MX-5 had fulfilled its intended role by then.

**Built**: 1976–82 at Billancourt, France
**Engine**: four-cylinder, 1218/1360cc
**Top speed**: 96mph
**Price when new**: £2,927
**Number produced**: 999,093

### Ugliest
RATED **8th** OUT OF **10**

Rotten as a pear,
and shaped rather
like a banana

## ON THE MINUS SIDE

You risked the condescending smirks of your friends if you bought a Renault 14, and they laughed openly when your gleaming new car's paintwork soon became peppered with rust. The 14 is one of those cars in which the smell of rotting carpets is an ever-present reminder of 1970s detail design standards.

# RENAULT'S PEAR-SHAPED FAMILY ROTBOX

These days, you probably perceive Renault as a design-led car company. With the unusual Avantime executive car, the top-selling Mégane Scenic mini-MPV, the acclaimed new Laguna and the erudite Patrick Le Quement, its design director, in its favour, the image is justified.

Yet Renault has had as many lows as highs since the Second World War: the cheeky 4CV was followed by the dull Fregate; the mould-breaking 16 came before the boring 12. And the Renault 9 – well, that was voted Car of the Year in 1982 and no-one nowadays can for one moment imagine why.

But have any of these low points produced bad cars? Not the very worst, true, but if I am to select a model for victimisation, it would be the 14. There are two reasons.

The first, obviously, is its dubious design. It was supposed to be aerodynamic and fresh, but its strangely curved flanks gave it a banana-like appearance. The car's technical significance was that it was Renault's first transverse-engined car, making it roomy, but it was always a weird-looking item.

There was something vaguely fruit-inspired about the Renault 14, quite apart from the fact that it rotted like a pear after a few short years.

And the second thing is rust: the 14 disintegrated faster than a choc-ice in a heatwave, making it one of the key used cars to avoid in the early 1980s – despite the longevity and eagerness of the engines, which came from a joint-venture (with Peugeot) factory at Douvrin.

Unwittingly, Renault even hinted at the rotten core of its small family hatchback in its advertising. One of the first ad campaigns for the 14 compared its rounded shape to that of a pear. . . .

Best Selling

RATED 5th OUT OF 10

Sold: 999,093

The 14, like all Renaults, came in a wide variety of trim and equipment levels; this one is the 14GTL.

## ON THE PLUS SIDE

While the Volkswagen Golf was uncompromisingly square-cut, Renault went for a softer image for its rival offering. The French liked the 14 so much they displayed one in the Pompidou Centre in Paris. Pleasant and responsive to drive with plenty of space for passengers and luggage, and good ride quality.

The interior of the 14 was roomy and comfortable, but the plastic materials used were apt to look rather motheaten after a surprisingly short time.

## THE ROVER 800 MKI
### AT A GLANCE

**Built**: 1986–91 at Cowley, Oxford
**Engine**: four-cylinder, 1994; six-cylinder, 2594/2675cc
**Top speed**: 131mph
**Price when new**: £18,795
**Number produced**: 221,227

Some of the original Rover 800 line-up, left to right the plush Sterling, the 820i and the 820Si: they were big cars but pretty bland looking and with lousy engines.

# CANINE CONUNDRUM – Q: WAS THE ROVER 800 A DOG? (A: YES)

If you thought I was cruel to the car on the previous page then you might not want to read this. The original Rover 800 is a bad car – there, I've said it.It's one of those models that the critics of the time seemed to endorse; lots of headlines with 'British' and 'world-beater' in them.

We'll leave aside the featureless, anodyne styling (it was feted in 1986 but I am at a loss as to why, unless criticism was seen as being unpatriotic). And we won't major on the early choice of a Honda-sourced 2.5-litre V6 engine, where its torquey nature was at odds with the car's limousine pretensions, or Rover's own M16 twin-cam 2-litre with its none-too-happy reputation.

No, the real bad part only became apparent once the car had left the showroom. The 800 had an appalling record for electric and build quality maladies, with exasperated technicians having to pull apart the stick-on wood dashboard and delve around trying to sort out faulty senders, wiring, connections and other fiddly problems. And the car would never go back together again properly. This might have been okay under warranty, but once an 800 owner was out of that haven he was on his own.

**Fastest**
RATED **3rd** OUT OF **10**

Max speed: 131 mph

**Most Unreliable**
RATED **8th** OUT OF **10**

Awful engines and a real head-scratcher for auto electricians

British police forces used to love the powerful and controllable Rover 3500 SD1; they tried the 800 – this is West Mercia's 825i – but few were convinced by its performance.

The original 800 was jointly-developed with Honda (its version was the Legend), and Rover built both at its Cowley plant. It's significant that Honda's bustling factory in nearby Swindon was first established as a 'pre-delivery inspection' centre for cars like the Legend – presumably where all the Rover-initiated faults were painstakingly expunged.

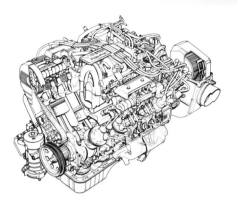

2.5 LITRE V6

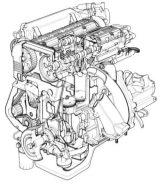

2 LITRE TWIN-CAM

Here are the two original powerplants fitted to the Rover 800, neither of which were highly rated and both helping to give the cars a reputation for unreliability.

Rover later added a hatchback option to the 800 and called it the Fastback. In Vitesse form, it was a fast machine.

## ON THE MINUS SIDE

You might have thought that, after 15 years of launching bad cars, Rover would get the 800 right from day one. It didn't. The car garnered a terrible reputation for reliability, build quality, and a pair of awful engines, which helped make the 800 a real no-no in the used car arena.

## ON THE PLUS SIDE

The 800 is not without its drawbacks but it was still a fine motor in many ways. As a used car buy, it made sense if all the niggles had been ironed out, and was good as a long-distance tourer for tall drivers. A 1992 styling revamp also added in some character.

Rover always intended to offer a two-door coupe version of the 800, but it only emerged in 1992 as part of a vastly improved range, and few were sold.

## THE SEAT MARBELLA
### AT A GLANCE

**Built**: 1988–97 in Barcelona, Spain
**Engine**: four-cylinder, 843/903cc
**Top speed**: 83mph
**Price when new**: £3,799
**Number produced**: unknown

### ON THE MINUS SIDE

Slow, crude and cramped, the Marbella was already ancient when it came to Britain in 1991 and the Arosa that replaced it was a world away in terms of sophistication. Flimsy construction (the Panda was designed in the 1970s, remember) means a Marbella is not a great place to have a big shunt.

# CRUDE HOLIDAY HIRE CAR IS BEST LEFT AT THE AIRPORT

Seats of the 1980s are a real mixed bag, unlike today, where they're all based on sound Volkswagen underpinnings but with rather more rakish bodywork. Until 1985, the Spanish manufacturer built nothing but Fiats, although they were often modified for local consumption – Spanish motorists, for some reasons, clamoured for five doors on their Fiat 850s and 127s. The relationship began to fall apart, though, in the early 1980s when Seat chose to go it alone and design its own car with the help of Porsche and Ital Design. This was the first Ibiza. Eventually Volkswagen stepped in in 1982 and turned Seat into its southern European outpost.

In 1997, Seat gave Spain the smart, economical runabout it wanted in the shape of the Arosa small car. Up to that point, however, the last Fiat-based model had staggered on to fulfil that role. This was the Marbella.

It was the Fiat Panda, Spanish-style, way past its pensionable age, and by no means a watchword for quality. It had been built by Seat in one form or another since 1980, but the 1988 Marbella version had gained a slightly more slanted nose, different plastic bits and a mildly altered interior.

Most Handy

RATED **9th** OUT OF **10**

Spanish tin box makes for cheap and cheerful hire car

Just about bearable as a super-cheap holiday hire car, the spine-jarring Seat Marbella wasn't quite as acceptable back home.

Dragging the old Fiat Panda-based Marbella kicking and screaming into the 1990s, Seat fitted a catalytic converter to its asthmatic engine, and called it the Micro-Cat.

## ON THE PLUS SIDE

The Marbella may be old but that doesn't alter the fact that it's a tough and simple thing, with low economy and all the Giugiaro design practicality that made its Panda cousin such a Europe-wide success (and don't forget, the Panda itself is still selling strongly in France and Italy).

While the Italian-made Panda gained an extra lease of life from new overhead-camshaft 'FIRE' engines, the Marbella made do with the old and ashmatic pushrod units.

None of which mattered when hiring one for a rock-bottom price at Spanish holiday hotspots. But, as the Marbella came to the UK, it was worth knowing what a crude little machine you were getting. The van version gave a clue: it was called the Terra. . . .

Seat started making licence-built Pandas in 1980, and this is one of the first. Shortly afterwards, Fiat and Seat fell out, and the Spanish firm was eventually bought by Volkswagen.

The unfortunately named Terra, a basic little van version of the Marbella, was also available in a passenger-carrying format like this.

France's very own answer to the Ford Cortina and Hillman Hunter, was the Simca 1301, shown here, and later 1501 – dull family saloons with none of the design flair of Citroën or Renault.

# CONVENTIONAL, MOI? MEET FRANCE'S CORTINA CLONE

Just as we Brits think of Parisians as either bike-mounted onion-sellers or else dark-haired, Beatrice Dalle-like temptresses, so the French think of us as Mini-driving hippies or *Carry On . . .* film extras. Likewise, for years, the Cortina-driving motorist was considered to be a uniquely British creature when, in fact, France had its own stratum of motorists who were exactly the same.

They did not bumble around the roads of France in a curvy, offbeat 2CV, muttering 'Zut Alors' and shrugging while puffing on a Gitanes. They plodded along, no doubt towing a caravan and wearing the French equivalent of a Pork Pie hat, at the wheel of a Simca.

Simcas are the long-forgotten squares of the French motoring scene, owned outright by America's Chrysler after 1970 and a sort of equivalent to our own Rootes Group. So while Rootes had its Cortina-copier, the Hillman Hunter, Simca had its own utterly conventional saloon, the 1301/1501 series.

Engine in the front, drive to the rear wheels, 1.3 or 1.5 engines, a useful estate version – here was France's Cortina in all its nondescript glory, as totally conventional as church on a Sunday morning, only slightly less absorbing.

The cars were based on Simca's 1963 1300/1500, only longer, sleeker and with somewhat more luggage capacity.

They totally failed to make an impact in the UK, and with so many devastatingly ordinary British cars to choose from, it's not hard to see why. The few that were sold here soon began to merrily rust away, and what was left of Simca was first transformed into Chrysler Europe, then Talbot, and then absorbed into Peugeot.

*Simca later added an estate car version too, as well as designing a new grille – exciting stuff.*

*The Simca 1300, from which the bigger cars were developed, was, if anything, even more boring – it was certainly slower and couldn't carry as much luggage.*

## ON THE PLUS SIDE

You know exactly where you are with these dependable old Simcas – they're easy to own, easy to drive, and easy to fix (if the dreaded rust hasn't taken hold). And, after all, Citroën sales only took off after it abandoned its trademark quirkiness for the conventional engineering of its Peugeot parent.

## THE SKODA ESTELLE
### AT A GLANCE

**Built**: 1977–90 in Mlada Boleslav, Czechoslovakia
**Engine**: four-cylinder, 1046/1174/1289cc
**Top speed**: 93mph
**Price when new**: £1,549
**Number produced**: 1,379,750

Best Selling
RATED **2nd** OUT OF **10**
Sold: 1,379,050

### ON THE MINUS SIDE

Like so many Communist-era cars of the 1970s, the Skoda was severely lacking. In this case, it was in the roadholding department, making the Estelle a dangerous on-the-limit machine for those with anything less than rally driver skills. It was still cheap, though, which is why we bought it.

Of course, there's no engine under that bonnet – just an inconveniently limited amount of cargo space – because it's, er, in the boot.

# WAYWARD CZECH ENDEARED ITSELF WITH CUT-PRICE ZEAL

With the Moskvich and the Reliant Robin mauled in the mid-1970s, the media had got its claws into the car industry. And the Skoda Estelle was an obvious next target.

The Estelle was launched in 1977, and instantly became a target after consumers' groups forced the Department of Transport to look into its wayward handling. This was caused by a heavy, rear-mounted engine and the consequently severe oversteer when cornering swiftly.

In 1979, a modified rear suspension including a less narrow track and wider wheels cured the problem in anything but extreme conditions (i.e. hooligan driving), but the Skoda Estelle was a tarnished commodity from that point on.

An early Skoda Estelle undergoing testing at the company's test track – they might've gone through the motions but didn't sort the car's dangerous road manners.

Not that that stopped it from being a steady seller in the UK. The stand-up comedians had plenty of scope for what became known nationally as 'Skoda jokes', but the cars continued to sell on their low, low prices. Indeed, the British importer and car magazine road-testers tried to turn the handling deficiency to their advantage by advertising the Rapid coupe version as identical to the Porsche 911 in every aspect except price and power.

A seemingly bewildering range actually boiled down to two engines and two bodystyles, with a British-originated convertible version of the Rapid also on offer for those seeking cheap open motoring. The last rear-engined Skoda was built in 1990, after which point the front-engined, front-wheel drive Favorit took over. After decades of Soviet rule, this was just the sort of modern car the poor, downtrodden Czech driver was after. Since Volkswagen took over, and poured in billions of Deutschmarks of investment, the company hasn't looked back.

For British buyers, the old Estelle-based range was constantly fettled to keep it fresh; this all-white horror is a 1986 Skoda 130 Rapid Coupé.

The poor Czech motorist, in 1970s Iron Curtain days, didn't have much choice in new cars, allowing Skoda to sell 1m of its rear-engined S110 cars.

### ON THE PLUS SIDE

Of all the East European cars of its time, the Skoda Estelle at least possessed some engineering integrity, and the factory – despite limited resources – revealed itself to be all too willing to make amends. The Porsche comparison wasn't too far-fetched, either: in the right hands, the Rapid coupé was, ahem, entertaining.

The 1959 Felicia convertible and its 1994 namesake – both cars being front-engined, unlike the two generation of Skoda models that separate them.

**Built**: 1956–57 in Coventry, West Midlands

**Engine**: four-cylinder, 2088cc

**Top speed**: 90mph

**Price when new**: £1,231

**Number produced**: 901

### ON THE MINUS SIDE

Even as classic cars, Standard Vanguards are heavy-going and hard to get excited about, and the Sportsman is anything but athletic despite its two carbs. A facelift of the III by Michelotti in 1957 at least tidied up the dumpy looks, but this was one 'special' that was anything but.

# SPORTSMAN JUST WASN'T CRICKET FOR IMAGE-CONSCIOUS STANDARD

Today, car makers conjure up 'limited editions' of slow-selling products by thinking of a breezy name, sticking on some correspondingly lurid decals, installing a slightly better radio, and shouting the super low price from the rooftops.

The 1956 Standard Vanguard III Sportsman would appear to be a primitive version of such snappy sales techniques. But it isn't.

It's an uncomfortable reminder that Standard was, by that time, getting mighty unhappy with its name. Instead of implying regal flag-flying, 'Standard' was starting to be a metaphor for ordinary, dull, feature-less – bog, even.

This deluxe version of the Standard Vanguard III saloon, with its unique grille, two-tone paintwork, twin carburettors and overdrive, was intended to carry the altogether more dynamic sounding Triumph name – a marque Standard had bought in 1945 and rejuvenated with Standard-based cars like the Renown and Mayflower.

Standard's Coventry factory in full swing in about 1955, although some of the workforce don't seem too happy to see the cameraman

The car that was so nearly a Triumph – the Standard Vanguard Sportsman had a unique grille, a snappy duo-tone paint job and twin carbs for the traffic light grand prix.

The Coventry company got as far as ordering hundreds of Triumph radiator badges featuring a stylised globe for the car before its decision makers bottled out and decided to keep the car as Standard as possible.

Maybe it was a good thing to reserve the Triumph brand for more sporting material; the first Vanguard, introduced in 1947, was never any great shakes – it was an unreliable weakling compared to American cars in the rough, ex-Colonial markets at which it was aimed. The Vanguard III, which made its debut in 1955, was mostly kept alive by fleet orders from value-conscious organisations like the RAF.

Sportsman sales were terrible, just 901 in two years, perhaps because of the car's high price.

The dithering was over by 1963 when the Standard name, aged 60, was replaced forever by Triumph.

## ON THE PLUS SIDE

With its dandyish two-tone paint job, boosted performance, bigger brakes and two-speed wipers, this was the best of the early Vanguard IIIs. It was a distinctive British saloon from an era before outside design consultants made their mark, and British cars began to look like those from everywhere else.

This is a plain Vanguard III, not a Sportsman, but our young Lucie Clayton graduate here doesn't care and is showing us how to exit the car while employing maximum deportment.

**Built**: 1976–c1978

**Engine**: four-cylinder, 848-1275cc

**Top speed**: 100mph

**Price when new**: £385 (as a kit)

**Number produced**: 30

Worst Selling

RATED **7th** OUT OF **10**

Amount Sold: 30

Barry Stimson's bonkers Scorcher in all its glory: the strange concept foxed the DVLA, which classified it as a motorbike and sidecar.

# PHEW, WHAT A SCORCHER FROM BARRY'S RESTLESS IMAGINATION

Any idea what this is? Britain's licensing authorities weren't exactly sure when they first clapped eyes on the Stimson Scorcher in 1976, hesitatingly classifying it as a motorcycle-sidecar combination.

By law that meant 'rider' and 'pillion' had to wear crash helmets but the third occupant – the Scorcher seated three in a row – was legally the sidecar occupant and, thus, could ride bareheaded.

However, designer Barry Stimson, who designed the car in France, advised any trio of Scorcher occupants to wear skid-lids because his outrageous trike, with Mini subframe, engine and gearbox at the front, could touch a giddy 100mph at full tilt.

The plastic body, on which driver and passengers sat astride, was made of glassfibre and the engine was completely exposed, hot-rod style – unless you plumped for the optional plastic bonnet.

## ON THE MINUS SIDE

Daft idea for a motorbike-cum-sports car that, from a legal viewpoint, is almost impossible to classify. Ridiculously fast even with the smallest BMC A Series engine, and bound to lead to numerous 'pulls' by the police, for both curiosity and admonishment reasons. Would you trust one you hadn't built yourself?

Mr Stimson was one of the doyens of the burgeoning British kit car scene of the mid-1970s. Hard-up enthusiasts could build an interesting sports car using the kit and parts from, say, an MoT failure 'donor' car. His first design was the Mini Bug, a Mini-powered beach buggy kit launched in 1970, but the introduction of VAT three years later killed off the cost-sensitive kit car trade. He finally gave up in 1986 after several more designs and having sold about 300 kits.

A Brighton company called Noovoh Developments sold the Scorcher as a kit car for £385 that could be carried home on a normal roofrack before you set about assembling it. Only 30 were made in four years and today, among the classic kit car 'intelligentsia', they're worth a small fortune.

## ON THE PLUS SIDE

Barry Stimson had the sort of active mind and can-do attitude so sadly lacking in the car design world of today. The Scorcher was unique in concept, loads of fun, and only dangerous when driven irresponsibly. Plus, it could be built and run for a fraction of the cost of a regular sports car, or big bike.

Not a happy landing for a pedestrian unfortunate enough to fall on to a Scorcher's front, but that exposed Mini engine gave the 'thing' 100mph potential.

### Daftest Features

RATED **9th** OUT OF **10**

Is it a car or is it a motorbike and sidecar?

Mr Stimson's diagram of the Scorcher chassis shows that the vehicle was at least well-supported in all the right places, which was just as well.

## THE SUZUKI X90

### AT A GLANCE

**Built**: 1996–98

**Engine**: four-cylinder, 1590cc

**Top speed**: 93mph

**Price when new**: £10,375

**Number produced**: unknown

# WHERE WERE ALL THE POSEURS WHEN SUZUKI NEEDED THEM?

The Suzuki Vitara, on which the X90 was based, gave just as much enjoyment with a mite more practicality.

The 'beach buggy'/fun car concept is one that car manufacturers return to time and again to brighten up otherwise dull stands at motor shows. But no car maker, apart from BMC with its Mini Moke and Volkswagen's 181 (neither of them very successful), has ever put one into production. Well, apart from Suzuki that is.

True to form, it showed a Vitara-based two-seater fun car at the Tokyo Motor Show in 1991, presumably in a bad year for new product. No-one thought any more about it until, five years later and after much deliberation, the Japanese company announced the X90 would be going on sale.

It had done its sums and calculated that it would be just the thing for the Californian sun worshipper – a four-wheel drive, two-seater coupé with lift-out glass roof panels and a generally funky 'attitude'.

There were, however, far fewer takers for the car, with its limited capacity for people and its even more limited capacity for luggage, than they had reckoned for. Only 7,246 were sold Stateside in three years.

Only two seats but, hey, when you're active DINKIES (Double Income No Kids) you don't need any more, do you. . . .

Lift-out roof panels were part of the 'fun' package aimed at sun-kissed Californian beach bums (or, of course, bottle-blonde Essex girls).

As seasoned market-watchers know, people tend to want an off-roader or a sports car, not a hybrid of both. There was a cheaper two-wheel drive edition too: as the car was already scoffed at by red-blooded drivers (that well-adjusted, completely 'adequate' bunch) as a hairdresser's machine, its internal lack of driven wheels made the X90 even more of a motoring figure of fun.

Around 1,500 came to the UK and, it's true, many of the buyers did tend to have both tans and blonde hair straight from the bottle, and inhabit that county just north-east of London.

The Suzuki X90 in its natural habitat: with a healthy and attractive outdoor couple at, er, a dry skiing slope somewhere in the UK on a grey afternoon.

## ON THE MINUS SIDE

Barmy two-seater off-roader (the four-wheel drive one, that is – the two-wheel drive edition is apt to get stuck on even gravel drives) that's slow, impractical and daft. LA beach bums gave it the bird and Suzuki wished it hadn't wasted its time and had stuck to the Vitara on which the X90 was based.

## ON THE PLUS SIDE

It's not often car makers are daring enough to put a pure 'fun' car on to the market, and the X90 was meant for show and not go. Laugh at it if you will, but it's a highly sought-after car today, just like the Suzuki Cappuccino baby roadster, and reliability is assured by Suzuki's reputation for excellent quality.

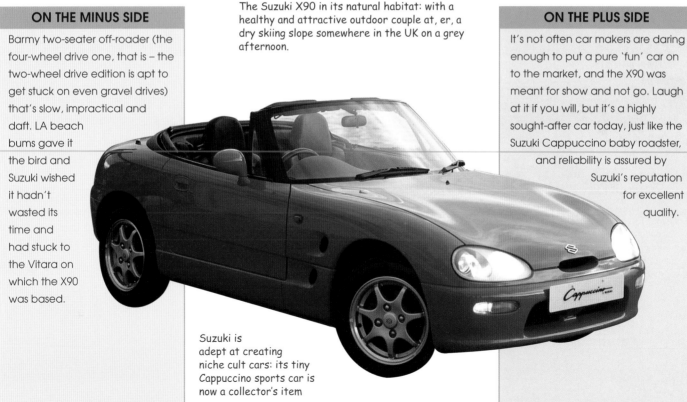

Suzuki is adept at creating niche cult cars: its tiny Cappuccino sports car is now a collector's item

## THE TALBOT TAGORA
### AT A GLANCE

**Built:** 1981–84 in Madrid, Spain
**Engine:** four-cylinder, 2165cc; V6, 2664cc
**Top speed:** 106mph
**Price when new:** £7,295
**Number produced:** 23,400

# BIG BARGE THAT EVERYONE WANTED TO SEE THE BACK OF

One dollar: that's the measly price that Peugeot paid Chrysler in 1978 when it bought the mammoth but crippled American car-maker's entire European operations. However, it wasn't such a bargain because, of course, it included all the debts and liabilities that went with it.

It also included the assets: factories in Coventry, Scotland, France and Spain; the Sunbeam, Horizon, Avenger, Alpine and Solara models – yippee – and an image with all the prestige and fizz of a Rotherham bingo hall. And there, at the very bottom of the tea-chest, were the plans for Chrysler's new executive car: the Tagora.

Under the revived name of Talbot in 1981 the bluff barge eventually emerged. Designed in Britain, and with either the rickety 2.2-litre engine from the old Chrysler 180 models or a hastily installed Peugeot 604 2.7 V6, the Tagora had all the aspirational appeal in the office car park of the gatehouse that guarded it.

In the Great Lead Balloons of Our Time league, the Tagora slammed to the ground in record time, selling a pathetic 23,400 in just under four years – that's about 16 cars a day across the whole of Europe. Middle management would have preferred even a base-model Granada with vinyl seats and no radio than a top-notch Tagora.

Peugeot was rather too busy closing down Talbot's Linwood plant in Scotland and re-designing the family car that would emerge as the Peugeot 309 to pay much

No-one wanted to know the Talbot Tagora, even in deluxe SX form shown here with a Peugeot V6 engine. Tiny numbers were sold and Talbot was soon history.

## ON THE MINUS SIDE

Terrible, ugly old shed that Peugeot launched only with the greatest reluctance – and its own V6 engine option – after taking on the mess that was Chrysler Europe. No company car cred whatsoever and generally cold media reception meant that the Tagora was doomed from the start. The wonder is that it went on sale at all.

heed to the Tagora's plight. The Talbot marque faded away not long afterwards, with the last Talbot Express vans sold at the end of the 1980s.

It had not been a dollar well spent.

The boxy, bland, square-cut design was off-putting, especially to Ford Granada and Vauxhall Carlton drivers used to a bit of US-inspired glitz.

The basic Tagora was an unlovely thing too, burdened with a 2.2-litre version of the engine from the Chrysler 180, another hopeless Euro-lemon.

# LIKE OTHER 1950S KITS, THIS ONE WAS GONE WITH THE WIND OF PROSPERITY

The home-build kit cars advertised in down-market DIY car magazines in 1950s Britain offered a little bit of ersatz sophistication in a post-war era still gripped by austerity.

They had a simple posit: the chassis and feeble engines of old Austin Sevens and Ford Populars could be laid bare and a new plastic body, invariably of a sporting nature, bolted on.

Then most of the old instruments, seats and wheels could be 'replumbed' so that, after a weekend or two's hard graft in the shadow of the air raid shelter, a determined amateur assisted only by a set of spanners and the odd mug of Bovril could create his own makebelieve Jaguar or Aston Martin for the price of a few tanks of petrol for the real thing.

The Tornado Typhoon Sportsbrake pioneered the concept of a sports-estate car 10 years before the Reliant Scimitar, and you could build it yourself.

Few offered much design finesse, so the 1958 Tornado Typhoon Sportsbrake caused a bit of a stir, with its low-slung lines and useful opening tailgate mixing sports and estate cars a decade before the Reliant Scimitar GTE.

It could use the innards of a past-it Ford, and Tornado was a successful enterprise with its myriad Typhoon, Tempest, Tunderbolt and later Talisman models. As they were sold in kit form, the manufacturer could not be responsible for how the cars turned out, and while many were no doubt professionally constructed, some of them definitely weren't.

Alas, although there was also an open two-seater Typhoon, by the 1960s and the advent of the Austin-Healey 'Frogeye' Sprite, such make-do cars were deeply unfashionable. Some 400 Typhoons were made; and of those a mere handful were Sportsbrakes. In 1964, the firm decided to concentrate on repairing crashed cars.

## ON THE PLUS SIDE

Bill Woodhouse, the Tornado's designer, set out to create a kit that was easy to build. The fact he sold so many is testimony to his skill. The later Talisman was a fully built car that was so good to drive and look at that Lotus once considered buying the project.

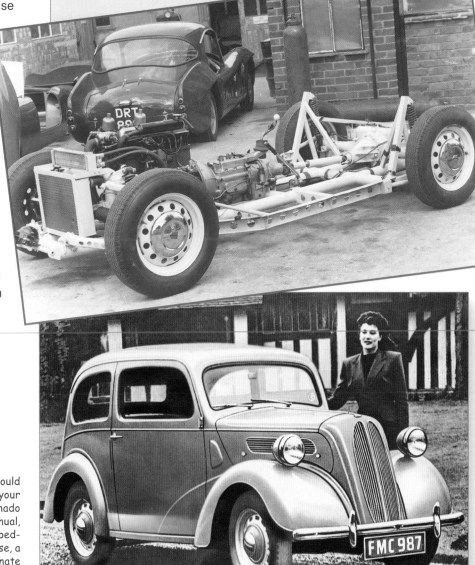

The basis of the Sportsbrake and other Tornado models was this professional chassis, meant to make bolting the thing together a piece of cake.

Most Unreliable

RATED **9th** OUT OF **10**

The instructions made putting it together so easy

Before you could set to with your wrench and Tornado instruction manual, you needed a clapped-out one of these, a Ford Anglia, to donate its vital organs.

**Built**: 1983–90 in Toyota City, Japan
**Engine**: four-cylinder, 1812/1998cc
**Top speed**: 91mph
**Price when new**: £7,981
**Number produced**: 225,700

# IT MOVED PEOPLE – NOT IN A WAY THEY LIKED

**W**hich car maker actually come up with the idea of the people-ferrying Multi-Purpose Vehicle, 'MPVs' or 'people carriers' as we all call them today, is a moot point.

Chrysler's 1978 'Project T-115', which emerged in 1983 as the Voyager, was probably the first vehicle designed from the ground up as an MPV, but the little-feted Nissan Prairie beat it to the market in 1992, and the Mitsubishi Space Wagon followed it a year later. The Renault Espace, which made its debut in 1984, set a new class standard for driving enjoyment and style. And somewhere in the midst of all these came the Toyota Model F Space Cruiser.

You only have to look at the Space Cruiser to spot its delivery van origins. In fact, although it used a truck-like layout, Toyota designed it expressly as a family car, with seven seats, plenty of cargo space and lots of comfort touches.

However, you really noticed its humble genesis when you drove it. With a soft ride but a high centre of gravity, and the driver perched van-like right over the front wheels, the handling was top-heavy and likely to pitch alarmingly in corners if they were taken at anything more than a stately pace.

Fortunately, with its initial 1.8-litre engine (later uprated to 2 litres), the hefty Space Cruiser

### ON THE MINUS SIDE

Bearing in mind Toyota's legendary thoroughness, it was a surprise it should enter the MPV arena with what was pretty much a van with velour seats. Apart from a few airport hotels, no-one was fooled, however, although the case against the car's horrid handling was never really pursued.

## Most Handy

RATED **10th** OUT OF **10**

It looks like a van but seats seven in velour-lined comfort

Sleek is not an adjective that readily springs to mind when staring at a Model F Space Cruiser, but there was no doubting the fact you got a lot of metal for your money.

Massive tailgate and handy sliding side door meant access to those seven, velour-coated seats was simplicity itself.

wasn't going anywhere fast – its 0–60 time was 16.2sec – and a press furore about the car's allegedly dangerous, tip-toe road behaviour soon blew over. Rather like, some joked, Space Cruisers themselves.

The all-new, purpose-designed Previa MPV arrived in 1990, thankfully making Space Cruiser travel a thing of the past.

The Model F Space Cruiser on the move: the thing was fine in a straight line, if a little sluggish when fully loaded, but top-heavy on corners.

### ON THE PLUS SIDE

If you like vans, and lots do, then the Space Cruiser will certainly appeal for its commanding driving position and vast space. Add in traditional Toyota reliability and an interior featuring every comfort and toy a driver could have wanted in 1983, and then it has an awful lot to recommend it.

Seems familiar – this is a 1986 Toyota LiteAce delivery van . . . which isn't exactly a million miles away from you-know-what.

The great-granddaddy of all people carriers was Chrysler's 'Project T-119', started in 1978 and shown here in 1987 Plymouth Voyager guise.

A Triumph Mayflower undergoes testing on rippled surfaces to prove its suspension's strength and make sure it was tough enough for export markets.

# THE ROWING BOAT THAT THINKS IT'S A STATELY GALLEON

There was just no telling Captain John Black. The ruthless boss of the Standard Motor Company, he'd acquired the Triumph name in 1945 and was determined to build new, Standard-based Triumph cars that were highly distinctive. They also had to appeal to export buyers, particularly American ones.

So his brainwave was to take the razor-edge looks of the magnificent Rolls-Royce Silver Wraith – the kind of British car that most Yanks wouldn't mind owning – and shrinking them to fit a tiny 84in wheelbase. It would create, he insisted, a city car that was also rather classy, and could be mass-produced while possessing a coachbuilt aura.

Well, the Mayflower was the result, and a more unhappy image of an economy-size limousine it would be hard to picture. Slab sides or what? Even a 1950 drophead coupé (a paltry 10 were built) failed to add much pizzazz.

Under those misshapen clothes, the picture was equally odd. It was, essentially, a small version of the Standard Vanguard, sharing its three-speed gearbox and back axle, independent coil-spring front suspension and hydraulic brakes,

Slowest

RATED **8th** OUT OF **10**

Max speed: 63 mph

but power came from an enlarged version of the pre-war Standard 10 sidevalve engine.

Souped-up, however, the car was most definitely not. It may have been smooth, frugal and easy to drive but it had difficulty breaking the 60mph barrier.

John Black would not listen to any advice about whether this really was the sort of car customers wanted – as far as he was concerned, market research was for wimps and what he said went. Predictably, it was a disaster in the US because its gutlessness made it tiresome on America's wide open freeways.

### ON THE PLUS SIDE

Quite apart from an unmistakable period charm, the Mayflower isn't bad at all. A hot-rod it isn't but its leisurely progress, smooth ride, excellent visibility, light controls and general air of good quality – not to say a surprising resistance to rust – add up to a cheerfully appealing package.

More arduous tests for the hapless Mayflower, this time a blast through a 200ft tunnel filled with dust. ensuring the car could cope with dirt roads in hostile foreign lands.

### ON THE MINUS SIDE

You can have a large limousine, or you can have a small economy car. The two don't mix, as the Mayflower proved. Overbodied, slow and bizarre-looking, American customers gave it a wide berth, and it sold well in the UK simply because any new cars were so hard to come by 50 years ago.

## Ugliest

### 9th OUT OF 10

Queasy mixture of the plebeian and the patrician

The uncomfortable lines of the Triumph Mayflower were a mixture of razor-edged limousine and suburban economy runabout.

## THE TRIUMPH TR7
### AT A GLANCE

**Built**: 1975–81 at Speke, Liverpool, Coventry, West Midlands and Solihull, West Midlands

**Engine**: four-cylinder, 1998cc

**Top speed**: 110mph

**Price when new**: £2,999

**Number** produced: 112,368

# LAST OF THE LINE SPORTS CAR RUINED A BRITISH INSTITUTION

The erudite Steve Cropley, editor in chief of *Autocar*, recently mentioned the TR7 convertible he once bought. He highlighted the car's good points – its comfort, its steering, its driving position and, on later models, its gearbox. He also recalled its 'limp' performance, which he cured (and just imagine how few people would go this far) by installing a beefy Rover V8 engine. After giving the car more power, he then realised its suspension, brakes and differential were too weedy to cope. So he fixed all those, and even reinforced the bodywork so the car wouldn't implode under pressure.

It was a graphic reminder of what an anaemic sports car the TR7 was. Introduced in 1975, it carried on the mantle of the TR2–6

This 1976 Triumph TR7 once belonged to ballet dancer Rudolph Nureyev, a man you might have credited with a little more aesthetic sense.

### ON THE MINUS SIDE

Pale imitation of a real sports car that flourished, for a brief time, because of a lack of any competition – there was only the Fiat X1/9 and the ancient old MGB. Where older TR6s had been gutsy, the TR7 tried to be trendy, and three factory moves played havoc with quality standards.

The TR7 made a surprisingly good rally car, particularly with the Rover V8 engine under its sloping nose. Here, Per Eklund is on his way to a second place on the 1979 Mintex Rally.

series, but did not extend their tradition of raucous hedonism.

Monocoque construction (instead of a separate chassis) made it smooth, but the 2-litre Triumph Dolomite engine and four-speed gearbox were the opposite of fiery. Flat-capsters hated the wedge-shaped styling, by Harris 'Mr Allegro' Mann, and it only came as a coupé.

The usual, depressing British Leyland development took place too late: a year's wait for a five-speed gearbox, three years for a soft-top, four years for a V8 engine (even then the TR8 was sold only in the USA), and never for an often-promised 16-valve engine.

Most discerning customers were quickly diverted by new-generation sporting cars like the Saab 99 Turbo and Volkswagen Golf GTi, and the TR7/8 ended the TR line for good. Even the patient Mr Cropley got fed up with his pet project and sold his, at a thumping loss.

Horsewoman Beryl McCain with her steed. Oh, yes, and a TR7. Actually, a bit more horsepower would have helped the early TR7 no end. . . .

## ON THE PLUS SIDE

You have to look at the TR7 in context: it was aimed at the USA, where the crude TR6 would anyway have been outlawed on safety and emissions grounds. Lots of good qualities, like a very civilised cockpit, and a late-model, five-speed convertible does have a touch of Jilly Cooper glamour.

Pop-up headlamps kept the nose of the TR7 trim, but a giant Triumph logo surrounded by winner's laurels was a bit previous for such a pup.

It could be a still from a hairspray commercial, but this is in fact a PR picture of the first TR7 convertible, which made its tardy debut five years after the coupé.

**Built**: 1964–68 in Kingsbury, north London
**Engine**: six-cylinder, 3909cc
**Top speed**: 100mph
**Price when new**: £1,995
**Number produced**: 6,555

Daftest
Features

RATED 10th OUT OF 10

Rolls-Royce engine
failed to restore
faded Princess

## ON THE MINUS SIDE

Dubious combination of
overweight BMC barge
and Rolls-Royce
military vehicle
power didn't make
for motoring fun.
With 18mpg and
Rolls complexity,
costly to run and
maintain yet
totally lacking
in Jag-style sex
appeal. There was
nearly a Bentley
version which,
thankfully, was
canned before
it tarnished that
great name.

# ROLLS ENGINE AND A ROYAL NAME JUST WEREN'T ENOUGH

'For many people', expounded *Autocar* magazine in 1964, 'the privilege of driving behind a new Rolls-Royce engine installed in a new model will be worth the [£2,000] price'.

The very thinking, indeed, that saw the British Motor Corporation cajole a wary Rolls-Royce into installing a Rolls engine into a big BMC saloon. It then managed to flog 6,555 examples of the Vanden Plas Princess 4-litre R in four years.

But considering the snobbish R-R kudos, that was pathetic: its forebear, the Vanden Plas Princess 3-litre, had managed over 12,500 in the preceding five. Likewise, it was based on the Austin A99/110, but was arguably more stylish – a Pininfarina original, no less, complete with subtle fins. The 4-litre had them shorn off.

Yes, but that Rolls engine, you point out: the 3-litre was saddled with BMC's heavy 2.9-litre Austin lump, after all. Well, it wasn't the near-silent wonder from the Silver Cloud but a straight six-cylinder 3909cc FB60 engine usually found in Rolls-powered military vehicles.

True, this engine, as Autocar said, endowed the 4-litre R with slightly more refinement and a higher top speed than the 3-litre. But, then, they were both mayoral-looking,

The stately profile of the Vanden Plas Princess
4-litre R concealed a Rolls-Royce powerplant,
albeit one shared with armoured cars.

ponderous-handling affairs hardly likely to appeal to the under-60s. And the 3-litre was no less woody, leathery or carpeted than its aspirant replacement.

A reasonable engine in a mediocre body does not a good car make . . . and the 3-litre was, at least, honestly mediocre all round. Little wonder Rolls quickly cancelled its own, Bentley-badged version of the never-repeated joint venture.

The earlier Vanden Plas Princess 3-litre was, if anything, rather more stylish with its Pininfarina-styled fins; still, both cars are a bit funereal.

In essence, the Vanden Plas cars were nothing more than cultivated versions of this, the Austin A99 Westminster, launched in 1959.

## THE VAUXHALL
## VICTOR F-TYPE

AT A GLANCE

**Built**: 1957–61 in Luton, Bedfordshire
**Engine**: four-cylinder, 1508cc
**Top speed**: 75mph
**Price when new**: £758
**Number produced**: 390,504

# TRUSTY BUT RUSTY, THE REP'S FAVOURITE WAS BORN IN LUTON

It's hard to imagine the fuss made about the unveiling of the Vauxhall Victor 'Estate Car' in 1958. But fuss there was: this was the first official estate car Vauxhall had ever made at Luton.

There had been Vauxhall wagons before, but they'd been conversions carried out by coachbuilders – in fact, several were produced by the makers of the Dormobile. Quality was usually patchy, and design, in a vehicle where practicality was its raison d'etre, not always thoughtful.

So a fifth door added a fillip to Victor sales. Lord knows, it needed one.

It was intended as a straightforward, 1.5-litre family saloon, with modern styling inspired by contemporary Chevrolet sedans.

Heralded as the first Vauxhall for world markets, huge numbers were exported – it was sold through US and Canadian Pontiac dealers as the Vauxhall Envoy – but only after customers had driven the cars for a few weeks did their inadequacies of quality and design show through.

Brits had less to complain about . . . until premature rust took hold, often within months. Among the myriad rust traps were exhaust pipes that exited through the back bumpers, and a 'dog-leg' shape of the leaky windscreen pillars.

Vauxhall's global ambitions for its 1957 Victor were obvious in its Americanised appearance; just a shame it was such a rust-bucket.

### ON THE MINUS SIDE

Luton rustbucket that, we were told, was a big export winner but, in fact, couldn't cope with life in boiling hot or freezing cold climates. And, of course, mildly damp places – like the UK – weren't much good for it either, as moisture forced its way (easily) in and got to work on the car.

Vauxhall churned out 100,000 in just over 15 months, and it became 'Britain's Number One Export Car' . . . until Johnny Foreigner cottoned on to its dubious quality. Surviving early Victors are, obviously, rare, and the estate particularly scarce.

The FB Victor that replaced it was considerably toned down in the looks department. It was better built and more powerful. However, the damage was done: Vauxhall's engineering and design reputation within General Motors was blighted – from the late 1960s, Vauxhalls were based on German Opel designs.

### ON THE PLUS SIDE

Britain was still a dreary, just post-war place in 1957, and the Victor with its snappy Americanised styling, bright colours and lashings of chrome, brightened the place up. It was a perky performer and – like the Vectra these days – put a lot of salesmen on the road to (one hopes) success.

In 1959, the Series II Victor cleaned up its act with smoother lines and myriad other detail improvements – all too late to rescue the model's tarnished reputation.

Vauxhall boasted that you could get four adults, two kids and 22cu. ft of cargo into its first factory-produced estate car; you could even have automatic transmission for an extra £25.

## THE VOLKSWAGEN 411/412

### AT A GLANCE

**Built**: 1968–74 in Wolfsburg, Germany
**Engine**: four-cylinder, 1679/1795cc
**Top speed**: 90mph
**Price when new**: £1,340
**Number produced**: 355,200

# REAR-ENGINED ODDITY WAS END OF THE BEETLE DREAM

There's a curious link between this car and the washrooms aboard Milwaukee Road Rail Company trains. It's the late Brooks Stevens. As a young designer, Stevens – who coined the phrase 'planned obsolescence' – was among the first to understand the merits of Formica. It made the loos of the 'Hiawatha' express trains he designed easy to clean. His distinguished product design portfolio soon included everything from Miller beer packaging to Evinrude outboard motors.

His passion, though, was cars, and he can claim some 46 different designs, many for Studebaker but also the Excalibur pastiche vintage sports car.

In 1970, the fuel-injected VW 411 LE was the largest Volkswagen you could buy, making it perfect for nipping down to the pub with friends for a pint of Whitbread and a crab sandwich.

The 411 estate, called the Variant, came as a two-door only, although its rear-mounted engine was an obstruction to really gargantuan loads.

### ON THE MINUS SIDE

Odd-looking family saloon with an air-cooled engine clattering away at the back, and the usual tail-happy VW handling. Okay, the Beetle may have been the world's best-selling car, but the 411 still looked as if it was stretching the concept just a bit too far.

Vollswagen had garnered its reputation for engineering excellence early, for example designing the 411's bonnet so that it crumpled up, and not back, in a frontal smash.

Few people realise, though, that he also penned Volkswagen's 1968 411. Like the Beetle, it had its air-cooled engine in its rounded rump, a 1.7-litre flat-four, but it could be ordered with four doors – a VW first – and as an estate, while the later 412 had a fuel-injected 1.8-litre engine, boosting power from 68 to 80bhp, and automatic transmission. The MacPherson strut front suspension was a big advance on the Beetle's system.

Trouble was, enthusiasm for rear-engined cars was waning, and VW struggled to sell 50,000 411/412s a year – chicken feed beside the Beetle's millions. The sensible but altogether less charismatic front-wheel drive Passat killed it off in 1973, and it proved to be the end of the road for the original 1930s Volkswagen concept laid out by the engineer Dr Ferdinand Porsche. However, you do still occasionally see the ungainly 411s and 412s pottering along, testimony to their Beetle-like propensity for reliability.

And in his dotage, Brooks Stevens must have been delighted.

## ON THE PLUS SIDE

Volkswagens had quality designed in from the start, and the 411 cars were no exception. They were spacious, practical and extremely reliable, and so what if they were anti-fashion – they worked. Their demise was the end of an era, and those who owned them were appalled at that.

An historic day: on 17 February 1972, the Beetle finally beat the Ford Model T's tally but rear-engined cars were already passé.

## THE VOLVO 343/340
### AT A GLANCE

**Built**: 1976–91 in Eindhoven, Holland
**Engine**: four-cylinder, 1397/1721cc
**Top speed**: 94mph
**Price when new**: £3,455
**Number produced**: 1,086,405 all
340/360 types

# MEDIOCRE HATCH FLATTERED ITS OWNERS BUT ANNOYED THE REST OF US

Volvo built over a million 340 and 360 cars – and a huge number of them ended up in the UK, where the car was a frequent visitor to the tail-end of the top 10 sellers' list. Why?

Because middle-class Britain fell in love with the Volvo image of solidity, safety and utilitarian style after many years' exposure to, first, the Volvo 121 Amazon, and then the 140/240. Antique dealers, country types, suburban mothers and Jerry Leadbeater in TV's *The Good Life* loved the capacious estates. Volvo realised it had something good to cash in on.

And how did it do that?

It bought Dutch economy car maker Daf, and launched Daf's new family model as the Volvo 343 in 1976. This was a car designed around an automatic transmission, Daf's famous constantly-variable Variomatic that used a toothed rubber belt to transmit power without the need for a gearchange. Consequently, driving pleasure came a long way down the list of priorities, which was headed by ease of town driving, with Volvo's characteristically bluff, sex-less styling a close second. Power came from a Renault engine.

The Volvo 343 made a splash with snobby British drivers who thought they were getting one up on Escort drivers by going 'Swedish', when they were in truth going 'Dutch'.

Struggling up the hill, the heavy Volvo 343, initially available only as an automatic three-door hatchback, was soon a regular at the front of slow-moving traffic.

Rear-wheel driven and painfully slow and boring, the 343 wasn't even that well made, standards being rather slacker in the Nether-lands than in Sweden. But it didn't matter: the punters were fooled and bought the 343 in droves, smug in the knowledge that it was a proper Volvo.

Later came a Volvo manual gearbox option (1979), five doors (1980), bigger engines including a Volvo 2-litre and a saloon car option (1983). But the image of a dull new car for smug old fogeys stuck . . . and Volvo boomed.

Developments of the basic design soon included a four-door saloon bodystyle, a 2-litre engine and manual transmission – and this Volvo 360 GLE Injection has all three.

## ON THE PLUS SIDE

In a world of Ford Escorts and Vauxhall Astras, the Volvo 343 offered a competitively priced escape route to suburban respectability. They weren't fast or glamorous and that was just fine; as sensible A-to-B transport for those too intelligent to get ruffled by Britain's hostile roadscape, they were fine.

## THE WINCHESTER
### AT A GLANCE

**Built**: 1963–72 in Fulham, south-west London

**Engine**: four-cylinder, 1628/1499cc

**Top speed**: unknown

**Price when new**: unknown

**Number produced**: 250 approx

### ON THE MINUS SIDE

Winchester claimed to have consulted cabbies as to exactly the sort of taxi they wanted, yet precious few of them were as good as their word and actually bought one. It was probably the herd instinct for the 'devil yer know' FX4 that put them off, rather than the Winchester's legendary slothfulness.

# RANK OUTSIDER LOVED ONLY BY FILM LOCATION MANAGERS . . .

Challengers to the traditional London taxi are few and far between. So the city's cabbies were naturally curious when Winchester Automobiles (West End) Ltd, a subsidiary of the Westminster Motor Insurance company, presented this slab-sided device in 1963.

The sober styling of the Mk I Winchester taxi was coated in two-tone paint; under the plastic clothes lurked a particularly slow and unexciting Perkins diesel lump.

Although the Winchester was slow, heavy (3,042lb) and underpowered with its 1.6-litre Perkins 4/99 diesel engine, it boasted one innovation: a single-piece plastic body. It was made of 'Cellobond', its supplier Wincanton Engineering said.

If your Winchester was smote a blow by another vehicle, its Cellobond body could be repaired in four hours using, it claimed, 'Glassfibre mat, resin, catalyst, accelerator, Sellotape and tin foil'.

Other novelties included an illuminated step for the rear passenger doors, and a sign that read 'Taxi For Hire' instead of just plain 'Taxi'. The MkI was painted two-tone grey as standard, the 1964 MkII came only in black, and the MkIII had an improved chassis.

But none of it really endeared the Winchester to London's sceptical taxi drivers, and nor did a later switch to Ford Cortina petrol engines to tempt the provincial driver.

This did make the Winchester popular with film location and prop men, though – diesel engines interfered with contemporary sound equipment. In almost 10 years, Winchester managed to sell just one a fortnight. The Winchester underwent a total body redesign in 1968, but the resulting MkIV didn't make any difference either: the city's cab drivers stuck steadfastly to the Austin FX4. There wasn't another challenge to the dominance of this doughty machine until 1986, when Birmingham bus and train maker Metro Cammell Weymann unveiled its Metrocab.

A total revamp for the Winchester in 1968 neatened it up, but the cab was still no threat to the dominant Austin FX4.

## ON THE PLUS SIDE

I've never driven one or been in one, so I can't mount an adequate defence of the Winchester. I mean, have you ever even seen one? Suffice to say its very presence on London's streets added to Britain's motoring bio-diversity, which is always welcome. Just like it for being different. . . .

## THE YUGO SANA
### AT A GLANCE

**Built:** 1989–92 in Kragujevac, Yugoslavia
**Engine:** four-cylinder, 1372cc
**Top speed:** 93mph
**Price when new:** £5,790
**Number produced:** unknown

The Florida was intended to drag Yugo up by its boot-straps, using Fiat Tipo underpinnings and Giugiaro styling – neat, if unremarkable.

The Yugo 311, a crummy hatchback version of the ancient Fiat 128, was the firm's product staple for years; the repulsive bodykit on this one, shamefully, is British-sourced.

# WAR IN THE BALKANS LED TO THE YUGO SANA'S DOWNFALL

'The cheapest new car in America' was a proud boast that turned sour very fast for its Yugoslavian maker in the 1980s. Sales of the Yugo 55, an ugly hatchback, Metro-size, were initially brisk, as blue-collar America jostled for a spanking new 'compact' in exchange for just a fistful of dollars. There was even a power-top convertible version. The entrepreneur pushing it, Malcolm Bricklin, had previously made a fortune selling first Italian scoooters and then Subaru cars, before losing it all on an ill-fated Canadian sports car venture.

But the Yugo's quality and reliability were so dire that irate customers soon clamoured for their money back.

Instead of returning the greenbacks, Yugo's solution was a new car, called the Florida, to salute a disenchanted American market. Well, not totally new, since much of its mechanical hardware was shared with the Fiat Tipo, but it did at least possess a neat new body, styled by Italdesign.

Quality was vastly improved, claimed the factory, but prices were still rock bottom. Critics in 1989 found it reasonable enough to drive, although they vigorously took issue with the improved quality claim – there were rough edges aplenty, and scant attention paid to detail design. It was sold in the UK too, as the Yugo Sana.

But the civil war in what was, by then, Serbia effectively ended any hopes of international success as exports were abruptly terminated – partly because the factory where the Sana was nailed together also had a lucrative sideline churning out arms. Certainly, no self-respecting Croatian or Bosnian would want to be seen dead in what was, anyway, an extraordinarily lacklustre motor car. And nor should you.

Bombs came and fell on the Zastava factory, stopping the Yugo Sana – as it was called in the UK – in its tracks; shame.

Yugo made a botched attempt to conquer America – hence this power-top convertible based on its Yugo 55.

# THE ZAGATO ZELE

## AT A GLANCE

**Built**: 1974–91 in Milan, Italy
**Engine**: electric, four 24-volt batteries
**Top speed**: 25mph
**Price when new**: unknown
**Number produced**: 3,000 approx

Slowest

## RATED 1st OUT OF 10

Max speed:
25 mph

## ON THE MINUS SIDE

Making these unsightly mobile telephone kiosks marked a low point in Zagato's long and glorious history, and there's nothing to link them to the carrozzeria's famous coachbuilt sports cars. As an importer, too, Bristol had no idea how to sell the Zele to us Brits. There again, who would have?

The curiously upright Zagato Zele, which helped the Milan coachbuilder through a business bad patch, was sold in the US as the Elcar, and in the UK by Bristol.

# IT KEPT ZAGATO GOING BUT DIDN'T SPARK MUCH INTEREST

You can make the most glamorous products in the world but, when times are tough, you either have to adapt or die. Zagato, the celebrated Italian coachbuilder, had been around since 1919 and produced some of the most beautiful and/or dramatic sports car bodies of all time – the Alfa Romeo 1750SS, Aston Martin DB4GT and Lancia Fulvia Sport spring to mind. In 1972, however, its work had all but dried up.

So the company designed this tiny, upright electric car as an emergency measure to keep its Milan factory humming.

Just 77in long and with a glassfibre body moulded in two, left and right parts joined along the centre, mounted on the tiny car's back axle was a Marelli electric motor that produced 1,000 watts of electricity thanks to four 24-volt batteries.

It translated to 25mph and a range of 43 miles. Revealed at the 1972 Geneva motor show but not on sale until 1974, it went down well, with 225 sold in 1975.

This 1981 Zagato prototype smartened up the little Latin electric car and eventually went on sale – although not here – as the Nuova Zele.

## Ugliest

RATED **10th** OUT OF **10**

A mobile telephone box might suit Superman, but not us

## ON THE PLUS SIDE

Obviously, it's no beauty, but the Zagato Zele – possibly with a bit of a visual makeover – could be just the thing for smoggy California today. Clean emissions and whispering quietness would endear it to the state's power-starved commuters and, of course, it could fit into the tightest downtown parking space.

## Most Unreliable

RATED **10th** OUT OF **10**

Don't stray too far from an electric socket

It was a hit as a trendy urban runabout in the USA and also came, briefly, to the UK in 1976, thanks to importer Bristol – for which Zagato designed and built the body of the 412. A tiny number was sold.

Zagato continued to make electric cars throughout the 1970s and '80s, introducing the bigger, more modern Nuova Zele in 1981.

Compared to Zagato's usual fare, the Zeles were an undignified joke, and by the mid-1980s it was back in the supercar business with the Aston Martin Vantage Zagato and Maserati Biturbo Spider. The company's electric interlude was quietly forgotten, even though its coachbuilding activities have now ground to a halt too.

## SLOWEST CARS

## MOST UNRELIABLE CARS

| | | Max speed |
|---|---|---|
| 1 | Zagato Zele | 25 mph |
| 2 | AC Petite | 40 mph |
| 3 | Citroën Bijou | 50 mph |
| 4 | Austin Gipsy | 60 mph |
| 5 | Bond Minicar Mk E | 60 mph |
| 6 | Daf Daffodil | 60 mph |
| 7 | Lloyd 650 | 60 mph |
| 8 | Triumph Mayflower | 63 mph |
| 9 | Fairthorpe Atomota | 65 mph |
| 10 | Hillman Husky | 73 mph |

| | | |
|---|---|---|
| 1 | Allard Clipper | With five on board, the mechanical parts tended to snap |
| 2 | Burney Streamline | Badly cooled engine meant the long tail could catch fire |
| 3 | Dacia Denem | Romanian workmanship in all its hideous glory |
| 4 | Invicta Black Prince | An advanced car that jammed itself into reverse |
| 5 | Jensen-Healey | Lotus engine is a dream, when it works properly |
| 6 | Lloyd 650 | Made totally in Grimsby, that centre of engineering excellence (not) |
| 7 | Maserati Biturbo | Rapid: that's the word to describe the rate at which it disintegrated |
| 8 | Rover 800 MkI | Awful engines and a real head-scratcher for auto electricians |
| 9 | Tornado Talisman Sportsbrake | The instructions made putting it together so easy |
| 10 | Zagato Zele | Don't stray too far from an electric socket |

## TEN FASTEST CARS

| | | Max speed |
|---|---|---|
| 1 | Panther Deville | 135 mph |
| 2 | Maserati Biturbo | 132 mph |
| 3 | Rover 800 MkI | 131 mph |
| 4 | Nissan Sunny ZX coupé | 128 mph |
| 5 | Reliant Scimitar SS1 | 126 mph |
| 6 | Jensen-Healey | 120 mph |
| 7 | Lancia Beta Coupé Hi-Fi | 117 mph |
| 8 | Lonsdale 2.6 | 111 mph |
| 9 | MG Maestro 1600 | 111 mph |
| 10 | Morgan Plus Four Plus | 110 mph |

## TEN UGLIEST CARS

| 1 | AMC Pacer | Goldfish bowl on wheels that's bigger than a Mondeo |
|---|---|---|
| 2 | Fairthorpe Atomota | Homemade lash-up with crude rear fins |
| 3 | Lea-Francis Lynx | Two cigars and a circular grille do not a fine car make |
| 4 | Mini Marcos | Not so much designed as roughly chiselled |
| 5 | Nissan Sunny ZX coupé | The dreariest-looking sporting car ever? |
| 6 | Polski-Fiat Polonez | All the style and class of Warsaw Airport c. 1962 |
| 7 | Reliant Scimitar SS1 | Droopy roadster with appalling panel fit |
| 8 | Renault 14 | Rotten as a pear, and shaped rather like a banana |
| 9 | Triumph Mayflower | Queasy mixture of the plebeian and the patrician |
| 10 | Zagato Zele | A mobile telephone box might suit Superman, but not us |

## TEN MOST HANDY CARS

| |  | |
|---|---|---|
| 1 | Austin Gipsy | Comfortable off-road alternative to a Land-Rover |
| 2 | Bedford Beagle | Bit of a hound in the looks department but a useful runabout |
| 3 | Dutton Sierra | 4x4 looks without the fuel consumption, and cheap to fix |
| 4 | Hillman Husky | Dependable little estate for the timewarp small business |
| 5 | Lonsdale 2.6 | No-frills Aussie barge ideal for cash-strapped antique dealers |
| 6 | Mahindra Jeep | Tough as uncooked okra but likely to curry favour in the wild |
| 7 | Matra Rancho | Pioneering, roomy leisure car with low running costs |
| 8 | Reliant Robin | Perfect for nipping around town with the minimum of outlay |
| 9 | Seat Marbella | Spanish tin box makes for cheap and cheerful hire car |
| 10 | Toyota Space Cruiser | It looks like a van but seats seven in velour-lined comfort |

| | Worst Selling Cars | Number sold |
|---|---|---|
| 1 | Owen Sedanca | 2 |
| 2 | Lea-Francis Lynx | 3 |
| 3 | Burney Streamline | 12 |
| 4 | Invicta Black Prince | 16 |
| 5 | Allard Clipper | 20 |
| 6 | Morgan Plus Four Plus | 26 |
| 7 | Stimson Scorcher | 30 |
| 8 | Rapport Ritz | 40 |
| 9 | Panther Deville | 60 |
| 10 | Citroën Bijou | 200 |

# BEST SELLING CARS

# DAFTEST FEATURES

| | | Amount sold |
|---|---|---|
| 1 | Dacia Denem | 1,500,000 |
| 2 | Skoda Estelle | 1,379,050 |
| 3 | Ford Mustang II | 1,107,718 |
| 4 | Volvo 343 | 1,086,405 |
| 5 | Renault 14 | 999,093 |
| 6 | Simca 1301/1501 | 905,098 |
| 7 | Austin Allegro | 642,350 |
| 8 | Mini Clubman | 473,189 |
| 9 | Polski Fiat Polonez | 440,500 |
| 10 | Hillman Imp | 440,032 |

| | | |
|---|---|---|
| 1 | AMC Pacer | Doors are different sizes, fine in the USA but impractical on right-hand-drive cars |
| 2 | Austin Gipsy | Rubber suspension failed to take all of the punishment |
| 3 | Hillman Imp | Engine in the back like a Beetle but without VW's high quality |
| 4 | MG Maestro 1600 | Ghastly talking dashboard |
| 5 | Nuffield Oxford Taxicab | One side open to the elements so driver has a constant cold |
| 6 | Panther Deville | Luggage stored in a fake trunk lashed on to the back |
| 7 | Polski Fiat Polonez | Hatchback yes but folding rear seats — er . . . |
| 8 | Rapport Ritz | Electric aerofoil raises when headlights are on, ruining aerodynamics |
| 9 | Stimson Scorcher | Is it a car or is it a motorbike and sidecar? |
| 10 | Vanden Plas 4-litre R | Rolls-Royce engine failed to restore faded Princess |

RTF 611Y

LEAGUE TABLES